CrossWords
for
Grief

CrossWords
for
Grief

GOD'S TRUTHS
FOR ENCOURAGEMENT
AND HOPE

SHARON ZEHNDER

Xulon Press

Xulon Press
2301 Lucien Way #415
Maitland, FL 32751w
407.339.4217
www.xulonpress.com

Printed in the United States of America.

ISBN-13: 978-1-6305-0487-8

DEDICATION PAGE

For Mark, my husband
   – You bring such great love and joy.

For Eric, Zach, and Charista, my dear children
   – You make my life rich and full.

In memory of Karen, my twin-sister with Jesus
   – I look forward to our future abundant life together.

TABLE OF CONTENTS

INTRODUCTION

When you need help, you turn to the right source. If you break a leg, you go to a doctor. If your roof is damaged, you call a roofer. *What do you do when your heart is broken by grief?* Where do you go? This book answers those questions.

I'm guessing you are bereaved or know someone who is. The death of a loved one profoundly affects a family and friends. How you survive the pain of grief is the primary subject of this writing. How it differs from other grief devotionals can be clearly seen by examining the Table of Contents, which lists 30 researched words related to grief.

The grief associated with the death of a loved one is a journey that most people experience at least once, if not multiple times. There are many words of wisdom in Scripture that speak to loss, grief, death, and challenging times. The best word is that any pain or grief is not the final word. Believers in Jesus have everlasting life that God Himself promised. It is a hope based upon faith in Jesus as Lord and Savior; He died and rose from death for us. God's Word, the Bible, is the only infallible source for understanding grief.

This book is a tool that will point you to God as He is revealed in the Scriptures. He has graciously given His written Word as the way He will speak clearly to you. The Holy Spirit uses words which He inspired in the Bible as His "now" Word. It is like He is speaking to you from across the table. He comes at the most needed times of grief and pain.

He is the Counselor who gives His wisdom and direction. He is the Giver of HOPE.

This book is a compilation of what I have learned about the most common emotions/feelings/experiences of the bereaved. This includes both positive and negative effects. Just as a crossword puzzle has definitions, you will see words with the appropriate definitions. I wanted to be able to research the deeper meanings of these words in the context of the Bible. That is why the book is titled *CrossWords for Grief*. These are words that don't come <u>from</u> the cross but will lead you <u>to</u> the cross. The definitions are based on my research of the Old Testament (Hebrew) or the New Testament (Greek) usage of each word. By understanding the meanings of the words in their original languages, you will discover new insights to help with your grief. Now you have 30 CrossWords that are explained in a reader friendly way for you to explore. The Holy Spirit will use them to help with your grief and pain.

Additional helps under each CrossWord include three things: written prayers, CrossRoads for Thought (various practical next step options), and other Scriptures. You can speak the prayers, choose an additional CrossRoad for Thought, or explore more Scriptures.

The 30 words that were researched were the result of a survey of the bereaved. Since 1999 I have worked as an Aftercare Director at a family-owned funeral home where I am continually in contact with people who are facing the grieving process. An anonymous questionnaire was given to 80 grieving people with 30 responses received. The 30 words are organized in order of the most frequent responses of grieving people who participated in the survey. The Table of Contents provides choices based upon your need for a particular day. For example, if you feel guilty about something you said to your deceased loved one, you can read about the word "guilt." It's OK to be honest about how you feel. I have a saying, "As you are real, you feel, and you will heal."

As your emotions are given to God, He will help you when you go to Him with honesty. He can lead you through all your discouragements and needs for His healing touch. The ministry of the Holy Spirit can reveal Jesus to you as Lord and Savior; He is the living Word. Jesus accompanies His people through their grief. If you know Him, you will sense His love and presence with you. When you don't sense His presence, believe that He is there working what is good and best. He promises that to His followers who are becoming grief survivors.

May you receive God's loving care for you as you explore your emotions, feelings, and experiences. May the Holy Spirit minister His truths to you for encouragement and hope all the days of your life. He is the Counselor who is sitting across the table from you.

That's my prayer for all who read this book.

BACKGROUND FOR RESEARCH

*W*orking as an Aftercare Director at a local funeral home, I am continually in contact with people who are facing the grieving process. Most of them have recently had spouses die. Others have had the deaths of children, parents, siblings, or other family members.

I chose to submit an anonymous questionnaire to 80 grieving people. I received 30 responses. This is what the questionnaire said:

*Reflect on what emotions you have had or experiences felt. Think about what that descriptive word is, whether it is a positive emotion/feeling or a negative one. For example, you could write down positive words like: hope, love, peace. Or you could write down negative words (things you have or did experience) like: despair, hopelessness, empty, purpose. That is what I'm looking for; it is the **one word descriptive answers**. Please list as many as you can remember that you could have used help with (or still could use help) in studying or having information.*

I asked the bereaved to respond in one word answers, as many as they chose to share, up to 30 responses. I asked for feedback on both positive and negative feelings, emotions, or experiences where they desired growth and encouragement.

After receiving the responses, I tabulated the top ones. The words that were stated as noun, verb, or adjective forms of the same word were counted together (i.e. faith/ faithful/ faithfulness). All of the top 30 words researched were mentioned at least four or more times. The top 30 questionnaire responses and the number of times each word was mentioned are listed in the *Appendix.*

THE 30 CrossWords

The following are the 30 words that were researched through Biblical resources. Most of the research was done with online resources of concordances, dictionaries, and encyclopedias. There are a few cited resources of printed books and online commentaries. However, I wanted most of the research to be from the root meanings of the Biblical words. If a Scripture is referenced, unless otherwise specified, it is cited from the New International Version (NIV).

It is not necessary to read this devotional from front to back. You can choose a particular word based on what you need for a certain day. Although my desire is that all the words will be read, they are written so that each word concept can stand alone for study. Thus, there are similarities and some repetitive concepts throughout the 30 words.

The words are organized in order of tabulated frequency responses. Each word is listed with a definition followed by a passage or verse that forms the basis of the writing. After that there is a prayer, three "CrossRoads for Thought," and additional Scriptures for study that correlate with that particular word. The purpose for the "CrossRoads for Thought" is that if God speaks to the reader through the writing, some appropriate next steps of action can assist in the healing process. The idea is that a reader can be drawn more deeply to our loving God who cares in times of grief.

CrossWords for Grief

1. HOPE
–expectation of good (Also HOPEFUL, HOPELESS, HOPELESSNESS)

Romans 5:5 *And hope does not disappoint us, because God has poured out his love into our hearts by the Holy Spirit, whom he has given us (New International Version).*

"*I* so want this to be over!" "I'm not sure I can do this!" Many times I have felt these ways. I bet you have too. I have kept it generic because it applies to so many things I've experienced...and I'm sure things that I will *yet* experience. The good news I tend to replay in my mind during such times is that I won't feel this way forever. I often will fast-forward 24 hours ahead and think of myself in a less stressed mode, the event or deadline being over. For example: "I have to go through a medical testing procedure for a few hours, and then it will be over." The preparation for it is not fun! But the procedure is done quickly. You get the point. I always have the hope and focus of a different tomorrow or a different time ahead. That focus keeps me enduring through the hard work and stuff in life I would rather avoid. It brings me hope for whatever is ahead.

I wish the fast-forward 24-hour principle applied for grief. It doesn't. If you are like most bereaved, you probably felt these same ways as you entered your grief journey.

"I so want this to be over!" "I'm not sure I can do this!" Your life can be so devastated by loss, death, and pain that this awful state feels like it could last forever. It is hard to imagine life ever being normal again. Life can be so hard that even living through 24 hours, let alone 60 minutes or even 5 minutes, can be challenging. Relationships and daily functions can be overwhelming. It feels like just the basics of daily survival are so hard. This can be reality for a season. You've loved. Now loss hurts so much.

So what helps to lessen the pain? Recall the word "focus." If you are a Christian, you have the gift of "focus" that changes grief. What is it? It's HOPE. Grief, for a Christian, has as its focus – hope. Hope, simply put, is faith directed toward the future (Easton, "Hope"). There are many parts to your "hope focus" but you want to concentrate on two: 1) the object of your hope and, 2) the result of your hope.

First, we know that as Christians the entire focus and object of our hope is Jesus (Colossians 1:27; 1 Timothy 1:1). Paul says in Titus 2:13-14, "While we wait for the blessed hope – the glorious appearing of our great God and Savior, Jesus Christ, who gave himself for us to redeem us from all wickedness and to purify for himself a people that are his very own, eager to do what is good." If Christ had not come, had not paid our sin debt, had not been raised from the dead, we would still be in our sins, separated eternally from God. Hallelujah! Christ is risen from the dead and lives as our living Hope, preparing a place for us, and returning to take all who believe in Him to eternal life in heaven with Him forever.

2

Our hope is rooted in faith – a faith in life that is given to us by a God who loved us and rescued us. Romans 5:5 says, "And hope does not disappoint us, because God has poured out his love into our hearts by the Holy Spirit, whom he has given us" (NIV). "Hope" in the Greek is *("elpis") - "expectation of good, hope, in the Christian sense-joyful and confident expectation of eternal salvation"* (Blue Letter Bible, *"elpis"*). "Disappoint" in the Greek is *("kataischynō") - "one is said to be put to shame who suffers a repulse, or whom some hope has deceived"* (Blue Letter Bible, *"kataischynō"*). Another way to state this is: Our hope is not rooted in deception. Our hope is in a joyful and confident expectation of eternal salvation, given to us by a God who pours His love into our hearts through the gift of the Holy Spirit. The good news is this hope is not something we expect for the future. It is based in a salvation that has already been won for us, given to us through our faith and belief in Jesus as our Savior. This hope is already living and active in our lives, carrying on with us into eternal life.

Since our focus of hope is rooted in Jesus, that brings us to the second point which is the result of our hope. Oh my, what results of hope abound in the Scripture. There are many, but let's focus on just one. We have eternal life. Titus 3:7 says, "So that, having been justified by his grace, we might become heirs having the hope of eternal life." We have the gift of life forever with God. While we possess this gift of eternal life now, we will realize it more fully when we pass through death into heaven. On earth we still have the pain, the grief, the hurt. In heaven there will be no more pain, grief, or hurt. There will be life forever as it was meant to be, in God's presence with no sin.

Do you know people who don't have this focus for their grief? How can they have hope without Jesus? They can't. Their focus will only be on the now. He is the author and source of all hope in this life and the next.

Do you know Christians who don't have this focus of hope for their grief? Could one be you? Who among us has not walked through the challenges and joys of life while needing time to refocus? Grief is so hard. But having periodic focus checks will help.

Focus on your grief expectations. Are you or others dictating a certain period to grieve? Don't try to set time limits for it. You can't be done with it in a specific period of time. You can't fast-forward 24 hours or for any other period of time. Grief should not be thought of as a journey that has a specific period of time to complete. Trying to do so can only bring exasperation and frustration with expectations either from self or others. This leads to hopelessness and discouragement. Please don't accept this grief thought expectation.

A Christian's grief journey can be all about HOPE! What you know in your head intellectually, can be lived out practically. You can turn the grief into something good working in your life. There are better days ahead both in this life and in eternity.

For a Christian, grief should be viewed as something to be experienced and changed for good, rather than harm. It does hurt – no doubt! While pain and death are part of fallen humanity, God uses them in our lives to accomplish things good and powerful in us. Grief is a process which is part of our spiritual walk. It goes way beyond what we would have scripted for our lives. In fact, I'm sure if we could consult with God about the plans He has in store for us, we would constantly be pressing the "Pause, Stop, or Delete" buttons. "No way, I don't want that in my life." "Lord, please!!"

But hope believes that the author of hope (Romans 15:13) can be trusted with the journey we must travel. Hope believes the fact that Jesus conquered all the pain and junk for us. He loves us so much, even being unworthy of His love. And glory days are ahead. He is the hope of glory (Titus 2:13). Knowing all this good news helps when focus gets blurred and short-sighted while living with day to day pain. Yes, it's real. Yes, it hurts. But the focus is on the now. Expand the focus to see the greater thing that God is working in you. He is perfecting you through this – making you more like Him. He can use you, even in the midst of your grief, to be a witness of the HOPE that is in you. Remember, some people don't have the HOPE; they have the wrong focus. They need the heavenly focus that you have. Share that focus with someone.

Oh! What comfort to know that your hope is rooted in God who loves you through it all (Romans 8:38-39). There is no pain, no hurt, no illness, and no grief that He will not provide the way for your endurance. Someday all believers will see Him and know as we are known. We will be with fellow family and friends. Our faces will focus on Him. We will see our HOPE! Jesus will be our focus. This short life, which may seem long, especially when we grieve, will all be worth it for the glory yet to be revealed. That's a heavenly focus, which bring you hope for any day. You can do this! By God's grace we can do this together.

Pray: I need a focus change, Lord. I know that I get stuck in just seeing the short-term perspective of what is happening. Some days the hurt is just very deep and it's hard to see any good from what happened. But I know that You have a greater perspective on what You are doing in my life. Help me to see beyond the pain, to focus on what greater thing You are doing in the midst of it. I'm so glad that this life is not forever, and because of Your love for me, I have an eternal hope. It's such great comfort on really hard days – a true focus. It keeps me going.

CrossRoads for Thought:

- *Who doesn't know your source of Hope - Jesus? Can you share what God is doing in the midst of your grief? If you need more hope, who can you talk to that has hope in the midst of pain?*
- *Look up instances of the word "hope" in a concordance. List the different types of hope or results of hope that you find. You may list: hope of glory, hope of salvation, hope of eternal life, hope of the gospel, etc. Read all the verses. Hope is based on truth. List any truths God is showing you to help you focus for your grief today.*
- *Reflect on times in your life where you needed to focus beyond the hurt, pain, or hard work to survive or endure to reach a goal. List each one that you recall. Now, reflect on what kept you going. What was your focus? How can you apply any of those principles that helped you endure or survive back then to your present grief?*

<u>More Scriptures:</u> Ps 146:5; Rom 5:1-5; Rom 12:12; Rom 15:4,13; Col 1:4-5; Heb 11:1

2. LONELY
–only one, solitary (Also LONELINESS)

<u>Psalm 25:16</u> *Turn to me and be gracious to me, for I am lonely and afflicted (NIV).*

I love games! Board games, trivia games, card games – most of them are fun to me. Competition, I guess. One game that I've never played is dominoes. What I have done with them is line them up vertically on end and made a twisting line with them. If I'm really careful, leaving just the right amount of space, I can get the last one in place. You probably know what happens next. A simple touch and they all come tumbling down.

Does it ever feel like all your support systems have tumbled down? One push of death and they all collapsed? Do you ever think that no one else "gets" how you feel since you lost your loved one? These can be common feelings which can intensify your loneliness. No one else totally understands what it is like to be you.

This is why I recommend that you start with those who have had similar types of loss. If you lost a child, try Compassionate Friends support group. If there was death by suicide, try a suicide survivor's support group. If your spouse died, try a support group for those who have become widows or widowers. Some support groups are educationally focused. Some are socially focused and are less structured. Each group will vary, but if you start with a group that has a similar type of loss, you may become more comfortable and less lonely.

Although no one can fully understand, God does. Trust Him to guide you. Jesus knows what it is like to be lonely. In His early years He grew up with a supportive mother and father. When He was near the end of His three years of ministry human support systems came tumbling down. Even the twelve disciples deserted Him. For a brief time He was deserted by His heavenly Father. All this was necessary for Him to take upon Himself our sins. As a man, He "gets" us. He was one of us. No one else can completely understand what that loneliness feels like. Only Jesus!

One reason I love God is He understands the needs of the most marginalized and most lonely in our societies. We see references in Scripture about those most marginalized, often listed in a triad – the foreigner, the fatherless, and the widow. There are many verses about not oppressing them. God defends their cause. A beautiful verse is Psalm 146:9, "The Lord watches over the strangers; he upholds the orphan and the widow, but the way of the wicked he brings to ruin" (New Revised Standard). The Lord watches over them because He knows that life is not easy for them. How lonely it must be to be a stranger in a land, an orphan, a widow or a widower. Perhaps you know this loneliness because it describes you.

In Psalm 68:6, it says, "God sets the lonely in families." The Hebrew word for "lonely" ("*yachiyd*") means *"only one, solitary"* (Blue Letter Bible, *"yachiyd"*). It is a desolate word. Yet is says that God sets the lonely in families. Is that true? Aren't there many lonely people out there who aren't in families? Yes, there are. But God has revealed the way to care for the lonely and put them in "families." It is called "the family of God" – the Church!

Perhaps, like me, you have had conversations with people who talk about their faith and love of God. They talk about them as personal. But they don't exercise the faith with any church. They have problems with the institution of the church. If we probe, we might find some reasons – hypocrisy, major hurts, disappointments of people letting them down, or those who misrepresent God's love. So they give up on the institution of the church; they don't need it, and they don't want to associate with it.

While it is true that a person can have a personal faith in God without the church, it is not God's will. It is not biblical for a believer to live as a lone-ranger with God. God established the Church, and Christ is the head of the church (Ephesians 5:23). God designed us to need and support each other through the church. There are many passages of Scripture referring to the body of Christ, the church. 1 Corinthians 12:27 says, "Now you are the body of Christ and each one of you is a part of it." There are parts (gifts) of the body of Christ that I can't have on my own because I need others. There are spiritual gifts that are given by God to members for blessings others. We see Jesus in others as they exercise their spiritual gifts and talents to benefit His church. We are helped and encouraged by the body of Christ because God uses His members to edify one another.

Are you involved in a local church? If not, why not? God has designed this to be a place where His presence comes to you and meets you at the times you need Him. There is the vertical aspect of God coming to you and affecting you through the spoken Word, worship, prayer and communion. There is the horizontal aspect of others being "Jesus with skin on" to you when you are most lonely. They are with you as members of the same body.

I know that even within the church the bereaved can feel lonely. You can get hit with pangs of loneliness that are the most intense and pervasive in this place of faith. That's why it can be very complicated even to attend church. All the memories connected with the deceased and the faith can be triggered through the music, sights, prayers, and rituals. Even surrounded by people, you can still feel so very alone.

If attending church was important to you and your deceased loved one or friend, recognize it will be different and hard at first. As there are many "firsts" and "seconds" and "thirds" etc., that can be challenging, this adjustment can take some time. Please be patient with your emotions and allow yourself to mourn the loss of your loved one or friend. What better place to be "real" with God than in His church? Trust Him.

If you have different worship service times, you might try attending at a different time. You may want to try sitting in different places. Be aware that this could draw attention.

There will still be hurt you have to go through, especially when you see couples, children, and parents. It is normal to miss the one you love. Others sitting in a church service who have lost loved ones or friends can understand what you feel. If you look closely, you will see the tears. You have fellow brothers and sisters in Christ who understand. You may not have identified each other yet. No one will fault you. Be open to sharing your needs to those who ask. No one can read your mind. They cannot know exactly how hard it is. Mention that you are looking for someone to talk to or a group to join. Someone can direct you to the right person if you desire more care resources. Some churches have trained Stephen ministers who are equipped to walk alongside to care and listen during a specific time of need. If you are a member of a church, those resources may already have been offered to you. But if not, please ask.

Do something either within the church or outside the church to help someone else. That is part of God's purpose for your life. When you look at another person's hurt and offer help, both of you are blessed. It's how God designed it to be. God can work through you to benefit His Kingdom. If you aren't sure where to help, ask the church staff about possibilities. By taking a spiritual gifts assessment test, you can discover where you fit.

The church is not a perfect institution. But it is where God promises to work and bless. There are other ways to combat loneliness, but if you are not connected or com-mitted to a local church body, this is where you begin. It will be the spiritual family God gives to you.

Pray: I feel all by myself! Family and friends do not understand how low and alone I feel. Surely someone else has to feel similar to me. I have no clue where to find them. I don't trust most people to come close to understanding. I've been hurt. I've been hurt by those in the church, too. You know, God, how I feel. Help! Is there someone else I can talk to? Hear my prayer!

CrossRoads for Thought:

- *One day each week do something different. Choose a different place to go and a different activity to do. You may try putt-putt golf. You may change your appearance with a haircut. Make it a point to talk to a new person at each place. Ask God to guide you.*
- *"Alone time" is different from lonely times. It is quality time. You can focus on positive things and goals. Think about some things you enjoy as part of your alone time. Examples might include meditation, planning, cooking, hobbies, singing, reading, etc.*
- *Check out groups – support groups, church groups, hobby groups, volunteer groups, exercise groups. Research them before attending to assess the likelihood of each group being a positive experience for you. Find a Christian grief support group hosted by various local churches through www.griefshare.org.*

More Scriptures: Is 1:17; Zech 7:10; Mt 16:18; Heb 2:17-18; Heb 4:15-16; Heb 5:7-9

3. LOVE
–affection, good will (Also LOVING, LOVED)

Romans 8:37-39 *No, in all these things we are more than conquerors through him who loved us. For I am convinced that neither death nor life, neither angels nor demons, neither the present nor the future, nor any powers, neither height nor depth, nor anything else in all creation, will be able to separate us from the love of God that is in Christ Jesus our Lord (NIV).*

*B*eing around children for a length of time means lots of questions. That's how they learn. "Daddy, does the grass hurt when you cut it?" "Grandma, why do you hum when you are driving the car?" "Mommy, why are there five toes and not three?" Sometimes there are easy answers; sometimes you are stumped as to how to answer.

It's not just little children who have questions. Living results in constant questions. Learning and then integrating that learning into our lives throughout adulthood is a challenge.

Questions certainly abound concerning grief. Things like, "Why did this have to happen?" "Why now?" "Who am I angry with and blaming?" Also, there are the "what ifs?" "What if I had taken him to the doctor the day before?" "What if she had stayed home that day?" Or, "How could he leave me so soon?" "When is this grief going to get better?" "Where is my loved one now?" Lots of questions, and like many others you are finding no easy answers. In fact, some questions have no answers. At least you've not found them.

That's right. Some questions have no answers. But sometimes questions change. You realize that the question you are asking isn't the right question anymore. Your perspective changes so your question changes, especially as you seek God's help in your deepest and darkest moments.

I love how God shows this time after time in Scripture. The Psalms are loaded with the Psalmists' questions and honest interactions with God. Take for example, Psalm 22:1-2, "My God, my God, why have you forsaken me? Why are you so far from saving me, so far from the words of my groaning? O my God, I cry out by day, but you do not answer, by night, and am not silent." Now if this doesn't clearly describe a grieving David, I don't know what does. David is desperate for God's help, but feeling His distance. Many bereaved people can relate to this honesty.

But even in his honesty, is David's question the right one? Has God forsaken David? By no means! David's expression of his feelings was not all the truth. It was *his* reality, but not really the truth. When you read further on to verses 23-24, David appears to have done an "about face" as he exhorts his hearers to praise God. Psalm 22:24

says, "For he has not despised or disdained the suffering of the afflicted one; he has not hidden his face from him but has listened to his cry for help." What happened between verse 2 and verse 23? As David approaches God with his deep questions, his heart changes and his perspective changes too.

When we lose someone to death, the questions come streaming in. We try to process them, each one, but some of them are so very hard. Some shake our faith to its very core. "Why, if You loved me, Lord, did You take my loved one from me?" "This isn't fair! Why did You allow this to happen to her at such a young age?" "If God is love, I don't want anything to do with Him if this is how He treats those He loves! Who is this God?"

There are more questions like: "She was such a good person, why would a loving God punish us like this?" "How can I trust God again after He permitted this tragedy to happen?" "If losing someone hurts this much, is love even worth this price of pain?" These may be some of the questions you have processed in your journey to understand your loss. If you have not reached answers for any of these questions, don't get stuck on one. The question may have to change.

Just like David, if you take your reality (hurts, grief, and pain) to God, you may see that He will change your perspective. He may even change your question.

How did this happen with David? Beginning at verse 3, David says, "Yet you are enthroned as the Holy One; you are the praise of Israel. In you our fathers put their trust;

they trusted and you delivered them. They cried to you and were saved." After spilling his heart questions out, David quickly acknowledges who God is. God is God – not David. God is the Holy One.

Here's where the truth of love comes rushing in. God is the Holy One, we are not. We are a people trapped in a sin-state, needing to be rescued. God came, in His Son Jesus, to rescue us out of that sin-state for His glory. We are eternally separated from His love without Jesus. Only God's supreme sacrifice of His Son, as the perfect substitute, could provide this rescue. Jesus, because of His love for the Father and us, obeyed His Father's will. He took the guilt, the shame, and the penalty for the sins of the world. Reconciliation is possible because of Jesus' sacrificial love. Eternal life is received by faith in what Jesus' death and resurrection accomplished for us.

Here's where love gets tough. If God had not done this for us, we would forever be eternally trapped in our sin. It wouldn't matter what love we had in this life. It would only be temporal. We would be eternally damned to hell. But because of Jesus' love for us, we can receive mercy (not getting what we deserve) and grace (receiving what we do not deserve). God originated this love. He first loved us (1 John 4:19), and He died for us while we were still sinners (Romans 5:8).

What love is this? Scripture tell us that "God is love" (1 John 4:16). It is His nature. There are several words used for "love" in the Bible, but the highest form of love comes from the Greek word *"agape,"* which means "affection, good will, love" (Blue Letter Bible, "agapē"). Vine's Expository Dictionary of New Testament Words describes the verb form of agapē stating, "of agapao as used of God, it expresses the deep and constant 'love' and interest of a perfect Being towards entirely unworthy objects, producing and fostering a reverential 'love' in them towards the Giver, and a practical 'love' towards those who are partakers of the same, and a desire to help others to seek the Giver" (Vine, "Love," both noun and verb).

Agape love is love in its truest form, birthed out of our God who is love, offers love, and then says He will show Himself to us through Jesus as we love Him and seek to obey Him (John 14:21). When life is viewed from this perspective, can you see how the questions we originally asked are changed? In humility, we can come before a holy God and say, "God, life, any second of it, is a gift from You that I do not deserve! How could You love me this much, to give me life and to give me love? You graced me with love for another when I deserved nothing!"

What is even more astounding is that this God, who has sacrificed Himself for you and me out of love, is at the right hand of the Father to intercede for us believers (Romans 8:34). Jesus understands grief because He was man as well as God. God understands grief as He had to sacrifice His only Son for forgiveness of sin. The words David penned in Psalm 22:1, "My God, my God, why have you forsaken me?" were later cried out to His heavenly Father as Jesus bore the weight of our sin because of love for you and me. Who better to understand love and grief than this God who created us and redeemed us?

Let me ask you some questions: Don't you think God can handle your questions? Your pain? Your honesty? If God loved you so much that He sent Jesus to die for your sins, don't you think He cares about you? Is life to be spent wishing for the past, angry at God for the death of your loved one? Do you know how great a love you have in God who chose to give you the gift of love through family or friends, if only for a season? Can you even begin to comprehend the love of a God that says that nothing can separate us from that love? It is all dependent on God's grace through Jesus who can make you a conqueror. Victory over sin has been won by Him. That is a picture of a love that you will understand fully in heaven.

We can join with Paul in saying, "No, in all these things we are more than conquerors through him who loved us. For I am convinced that neither death nor life, neither angels nor demons, neither the present nor the future, nor any powers, neither height nor depth, nor anything else in all creation, will be able to separate us from the love of God that is in Christ Jesus our Lord" (Romans 8:37-39). Now I ask you this question: "What could be of more comfort than these solid words of truth from God to you?"

Pray: Lord, I know that I struggle now because my loved one is gone. I know that some of my questions probably aren't the final questions, but I thank You that I can come as I am and You will help me. You can change my heart and change my perspective. I live thinking I deserve life a certain way, but I see that it is faulty, worldly thinking. I deserve nothing, but You chose to love me. Help me now, Lord, as You understand grief and the pain of loss. Jesus, hear me, today, as You intercede for me in my time of need!

CrossRoads for Thought:

- *Think of a person who best exhibits the love of God. What do you see? Spend some time in prayer thanking God for showing you His love through this person. Then write or call the person to bless him or her. (This could be a person you know well, such as a family member, teacher, or minister. It could be someone you don't know personally, such as a singer, author, etc.).*

- *Our hearts are changed when life is viewed as a gift of love from God, rather than something deserved that is taken away. Confess to God if you viewed His love incorrectly. Spend some time in worship with music, thanking Him for His undeserved love to you.*

- *When we love God, we desire to be like Him and obey Him. God promises to send His Holy Spirit to live within us as believers. How does knowing the truth that God lives within you help you as you journey through this grief?*

More Scriptures: Jn 3:16; Jn 14:21-23; Jn 15:9-17; Jn 17:26; Eph 1:4-8; 1 Jn 4:7-10, 19

4. COMFORT
–called to one's side (Also COMFORTING)

<u>John 14:26</u> *"But the Comforter, which is the Holy Ghost, whom the Father will send in my name, he shall teach you all things, and bring all things to your remembrance, whatsoever I have said unto you" (King James Version).*

I still remember the day. I was exasperated with parenting and my incapability to know the right thing to do with one of my children. In a moment of quietness I turned to the Lord in desperate prayer. I cried out, "Lord, I just need a counselor!" Immediately I remembered the word "counselor" was in the Bible. I proceeded to turn to the concordance at the back of my Bible to look up all that it had to say about "counselor." The verse the Lord led me to linger on was John 14:26. The KJV word "comforter" is translated "counselor" in the Revised Standard Version. I sat and prayed, realizing God had given me His Holy Spirit for help at just such a time like this. As I meditated on God's counseling me, I remember hearing the Lord remind me of something in my spirit that He had told me before. It wasn't about my child. It was about my sin. Wow! Big time curve ball! I wasn't expecting that. But it was very clear, that God was using this moment to counsel me about being right with Him before I could be right with my child.

I immediately confessed my sin and reflected on what I knew to be His truth.

I needed help. I needed counsel. I needed comfort and direction as a parent. People who love us hate to see us hurt as we grieve. They do the best they can to offer condolences and comfort. Sometimes the comfort offered hits the mark; many times it leaves us lacking or even in worse pain. People mean well, but as a society we do not know how to handle grief well with words or actions.

Good news...God does! It is precisely because God knows we need help that Jesus announced to His disciples, when they were troubled over the departure of their Rabbi, that they would not be alone. At the request of Jesus, God the Father would send the promised Holy Spirit to be their Helper, their Comforter, and their Counselor. The Greek word for "comforter" used here is *"paraklētos,"* and literally it means one who is *"called to one's side, especially called to one's aid"* (Blue Letter Bible, *"paraklētos"*). "Further description of this 'Comforter' or 'Paraclete' is one who in a court of justice pleads another's cause, defends, intercedes, and counsels for the defense. This Comforter intercedes and advocates for another" (Vine, "Comforter").

Jesus is addressing the future grief of the disciples over His departure. He says the Holy Spirit will: 1) be with them forever; 2) be the Spirit of truth, testifying of Jesus; and 3) teach them all things and remind them of all Jesus said. Let's concentrate on some practical specifics in this section that can help when you need comfort in your grief.

First, in John 14:16, Jesus tells the disciples that this Comforter will be with them forever. He says, "And I will pray the Father, and he shall give you another Comforter, that he may abide with you forever" (KJV). Although Jesus would be physically leaving them, the Holy Spirit, the Comforter, would be with them forever. Did you catch that? You are never alone in your grief, even when you <u>feel</u> alone. If you know Jesus as your Savior, the Comforter is forever with you. In John 14:17, Jesus says of the Holy Spirit, "He lives with you and will be in you." That is a comforting truth.

Second, in John 15:26, Jesus says, "But when the Comforter is come, whom I will send unto you from the Father, even the Spirit of truth, which proceedeth from the Father, he shall testify of me" (KJV). One of the challenges of going through grief as a Christian is the discernment of truth from lies. The enemy wants to lie about God and how God loves you. He twists the truth ever so slightly to prey upon a person when it is the most vulnerable time. The Holy Spirit reveals truth that will help discern lies.

Going through grief and loss is a time to cling to the truth of the Word. When you hurt and are finding no comfort or peace as you grieve, it is then that you should pray and ask the Holy Spirit, the Comforter, to reveal God's truth to you. God is FOR you. God loves YOU. God is working His best FOR you with His Kingdom purposes, even when you don't feel it. Anything that casts doubt upon this truth is not from God. Satan tempted Adam and Eve with a distortion of the truth in the Garden of Eden. He tempted

Jesus during the 40 days in the desert with a distortion of Scriptures. Do not doubt or question that he can try these same schemes upon you when you are hurting. He is the father of lies.

The Holy Spirit, the Comforter, will reveal truth to you when you call out. The truth will testify of Jesus. The testifying will be about Jesus who humbled Himself as a servant (Philippians 2:5-11) so that He could redeem sinners like you and me. This truth will be all about love, obedience, and forgiveness. If His love sent Him to the cross for you where He took your hurts and pains upon Himself, know that He now lives to intercede for you (Romans 8:34).

Third, in John 14:26, Jesus promises that this Comforter and Advocate will teach the disciples all things and remind them of all things He had said to them. I take great comfort in this verse as I cannot know God's Word on my own. The Holy Spirit takes the Scriptures that I read and reveals God's truth to me through them. Not only does He reveal the truth to me but He brings it back to my remembrance. Every step you take in reading and learning God's Word, entrusting it to memory or even reciting it aloud, is standing on a firm foundation for God to minister to you. If you don't know the Word, begin to learn it. Just start reading. Begin with the Gospel of John. God will honor your heart if you come to Him to know Him. By your coming to God, standing in faith and trusting what He says, you put yourself in the position for Him to give you what the perfect "Counselor" or "Comforter" can give you.

There are no better words for comfort than what God can give you when you need it. Who better than the Holy Spirit, whom Jesus sent to us, to minister to you? He will strengthen you as a believer, guiding you in your faith to the truth of the Word, always revealing and glorifying Jesus to you and in you. It's His promise to you. This Counselor/Comforter doesn't cost you any money. There was a price paid, but it was forever covered for you by God's great love for you in Jesus. Let's get this good news out to all! Free Counselor! Free Comforter! Paid in Full by His grace.

Pray: Oh Lord, You know me. I miss my loved one so much! I hurt at a deep, deep level that few understand. You know exactly where I hurt and what I need. I need Your comfort. When I doubt Your love, I know that is a lie from Satan. Help me be honest with You and trust that You will send me Your Holy Spirit to comfort me at times like this. I'm waiting with my Bible. Show me where to read, Lord! Open my eyes to see truth in Your Word by Your Holy Spirit's power.

CrossRoads for Thought:

- *Find a red-letter Bible, where Jesus' words are in red in the four Gospels. Take some time to read Jesus' words. Begin in one of the Gospels and read until you find a truth that relates to your grief. Write it on a card. Periodically, as you find more verses from Jesus, keep writing on these cards the words of Jesus that bring you comfort. Re-read these truths when you need comfort. Memorize those that mean the most to you.*
- *Look up Sermon 5, "The Comforter," by Rev. Charles H. Spurgeon, delivered January 21, 1855. This churchman writes about this work of the Holy Spirit to comfort. It is powerful!*
- *When God speaks to you of His comfort through the Holy Spirit, write it down. Did it come through the Scriptures? Through prayer? Through a Christian book? Through a professional? Call another person who is grieving and ask if you can share what God gave to you. This way you are sharing the good news of comfort and Jesus is glorified through your testimony. Praise God!*

More Scriptures: Ps 23:4; Ps 119:50; Ps 119:81-88; Jer 31:13; 2 Cor 1:3-5

5. EMPTY
–void
(Also EMPTINESS)

Ruth 1:21 *"I went away full, but the Lord has brought me back empty. Why call me Naomi? The Lord has afflicted me; the Almighty has brought misfortune upon me" (NIV).*

*D*o you know what your name means? And do you know why you were given your name? That information can be fun or interesting to learn. Sometimes children are named after parents or relatives who are no longer alive. Sometimes it can be a character in a book or movie, but often parents just like the sound of the name.

Naomi, an Israelite, was a mother-in-law to Ruth, a Moabite woman. Naomi's name means "pleasant." Yet in Ruth 1:20 Naomi tells the women in Bethlehem to stop calling her Naomi. She said, "Call me Mara, because the Almighty has made my life very bitter." That's what Mara means – bitter. Naomi said the Lord had afflicted her and brought misfortune upon her. She had been full, but the Lord brought her back empty (v. 21). Naomi had gone through the misfortune of having her husband (Elimelech) die while they lived in the foreign land of Moab. She had two sons who had married Moabite women, Orpah and Ruth. After about ten years, both of her sons died as well. She was bereaved of not just her husband, but now also two sons. All that remained for her were her two daughters-in-law.

That is some pretty significant grief! I have known friends and people I've met who had multiple losses occur in a short period of time. Life is going along at a normal pace and all of a sudden everything changes. Now it is so different. It might be described in a similar way as what Naomi said. Naomi described her life as going from full to empty. Hebrew for "empty" is *"reyqam"* meaning *"without cause, empty, in vain, void"* (Strong 108, "empty").

Can you relate? Are you like Naomi? Has life gone from a full, wonderful life to one that now feels empty, void, and you question whether it is of any value? Ruth, Naomi's daughter-in-law, expresses her love to Naomi and insists that when Naomi returns to Bethlehem, she is going with her. The period of famine in the land had passed and Naomi went back home. Notice that in Ruth 1:19 the women see Naomi returning after this period of more than a decade, and they exclaim, "Can this be Naomi?" I wonder if the pain of the multiple deaths of her family showed in her physical appearance. The stress of death can impact us emotionally and physically. I'm so glad that Naomi let us into the reality of her feelings by these statements she expresses to the women of Bethlehem. She's honest that she is bitter about her misfortunes and afflictions that she felt were brought by the Lord.

Is this true? Had God let Naomi down? Had she received a bad spin on the wheel of life from God? It is very common for the bereaved to struggle with God after loss. It is common to blame and question God. A person of strong faith before the loss can question even the worth of faith anymore. A person of no faith can question if there is a God. I'm so glad that we have a God who is big enough to handle our questions. He can handle our doubts and concerns. He can handle our complaints. Truly, that is what lamenting is. It is going to God in the safety of being yourself to the one you can really trust.

You don't have to pretend with God. If you are empty and void, you can tell Him. When you go to your Creator with the fullness of your pain and honesty, you can surrender to Him for ministry at the deepest places. You are running to Him and crying out for His help. Many of the Psalms are laments. The Psalmist begins with honesty and, in the process of venting his feelings, ends in praise. He recognizes that he is not God, and he declares the truth of God's attributes and works.

Did God let Naomi down? Has He let you down? You may have thought so. But what you felt is not really true. The truth is, as the whole of Scripture tells us, that we don't _deserve_ anything good. But God in His mercy _does not_ give us what we deserve. Instead, by grace through faith in Jesus Christ, He gives us the opposite. He gives us everlasting life with Him. Anything good is given wholly by God's grace. This life is temporary, but it can be enjoyed by the fullness of the Holy Spirit.

Do you live life that way? Do you wake up normally thanking God for the gift of the breath of life? For the gift of a roof over your head? For the gift of food to eat? I'd be willing to guess most of us don't. We tend to live life from a wrong starting premise. We wake up with the expectation that life should proceed along a certain way. We get sucked into the lie that if we work hard, we deserve nice things. We believe and expect if we live a good life and are good to others, we'll have a good, long life. Some even believe the lie that if we live a good enough life we'll make it to heaven. Therefore, when bad things happen to us, we cry "Why? What? How could this happen to me? Why did God afflict me?" Life can feel void and empty.

If you recognize a faulty premise, you can change and live life from a perspective of grace. This is a deep place of understanding that is key in the healing of grief. Start with this biblical premise: Anything good in life is viewed as a gift of God. You recognize that God lovingly holds your life in His hands and is molding you into His image. How well spoken by Job who endured the loss of all his family, and yet expressed in Job 1:20-21, "Then he fell to the ground in worship and said: 'Naked I came from my mother's womb, and naked I will depart. The Lord gave and the Lord has taken away; may the name of the Lord be praised.'" Verse 22 states: "In all this, Job did not sin by charging God with wrongdoing." You can be honest and express your pain, while recognizing even your very life is a gift from the Potter who is molding you. He is lovingly shaping you for His Kingdom purposes, which you may not see in the process. You can start each day by thanking God for His goodness. Therefore, when good things happen, thank God and others for them. Learn to replace emptiness with the fullness of God.

The best part of Naomi's story comes at the end of the book of Ruth. Her daughter-in-law, Ruth, ends up marrying one of Naomi's husband's kin so that her family line, which she thought had ended, would continue. Naomi had a fullness come back in her life that would be beyond her wildest dreams. She ends up being a grandmother to Obed. Obed was the grandfather of King David; and Jesus, our Savior, was a descendant of King David. Her life was directly involved in the coming Savior's descendants. That is the grace of God.

When you feel empty and life feels so void because of your grief, remember that God is working in your life through your pain. He gifted you with someone you loved and still do. Like Naomi, you may see life as bitter right now, but trust that as God had a bigger plan in place for Naomi, He loves you just the same and is working His grace in your life. Most importantly, you've been given a new name because of grace – Redeemed One!

Pray: Life has such a different meaning for me now. It is hard to feel joy or other feelings that are good. Some days I can barely function in thought or activities. Help me to come to You, Lord, and be honest about my pain. I'm sorry that I have seen life more from what I think I should have than truly from what I deserve. Help me to see that You have filled my life with grace, and help me trust that You are doing that now. Where I have emptiness, come, Lord, and fill me up with the comfort of Your Holy Spirit.

CrossRoads for Thought:

- _Read the Book of Ruth. It is only four chapters. See the change in Naomi's heart attitude in Ruth 2:20. Write any grace-filled thing (anything not deserved) that Naomi was given by God. See how many you can find._
- _Your life is not empty. Begin a list of things that you have that are good – that you don't normally think about. Be specific. Things like the washer, the shoes, the neighbors, your ability to read, etc. You get the idea. End this time in praise and thanksgiving to God as you linger over your list in prayer._
- _Choose a way to be kind to someone else. Do it in secret. You can send a written card, pay for another person's fast food bill, buy a gift card, etc. Find the joy of filling the emptiness by giving to another. Shhh!....don't tell anyone! It's a secret between you and God. Let God fill you with His love._

More Scriptures: Eph 2:8-10; Eph 5:17-20; Phil 1:9-11; 1 Thes 5:16-18

6. STRENGTH
–a defense, refuge, or protection, like a firm, secure fortified tower

Psalm 46:1-3 *God is our refuge and strength, an ever-present help in trouble. Therefore we will not fear, though the earth give way and the mountains fall into the heart of the sea, though its waters roar and foam and the mountains quake with their surging (NIV).*

*H*ave you ever experienced a tornado, a hurricane, or an earthquake? I've had several that have come close to me, but I've never really been touched by the full impact of any one of them. From what I understand, to experience one of these bad weather-related disasters is a life changing experience. It is a story that is eager to be shared by some who lived through it and survived.

Why? Why do people want to share and hear about these close-call situations? What intrigues others about these stories? Could it be the close line between the preciousness of life and the near-death experience? Prior to their accident, if my oldest child had not told his brother and cousins to put on their seat belts, the ER doctor said they would have been thrown from the vehicle. It was a precious life changing decision that allowed my family to survive. If your perspective about what is truly important in life is shaken by surviving one of these accidents or disasters, you walk away a changed person.

I'm so glad that the Psalmist included songs about the weather and the tumultuous times. He writes in Psalm 46:2-3 about the earth giving way, the mountains falling into the heart of the sea, the waters roaring and foaming, and the mountains quaking with their surging. Sounds like tumultuous weather to me! Yet, he says we will not fear because God is our refuge and strength, an ever-present help in trouble.

Can you think of anything that could be more fearful than seeing and experiencing the earth quaking, the waters surging, and the mountains falling into the sea? Clearly the Psalmist says that God is our refuge and strength in times of trouble like this.

Are you feeling like you have weathered a storm unlike any you have ever known? You have! Death and grief can leave a person devastated. Grief can zap a person of physical strength. This often happens with the emotional crisis at the death of a loved one. The emotional affects the physical. Extreme tiredness can set in, along with a lack of energy. Sleep can be disrupted and out of sorts for a season. People who normally are highly functional can become very frustrated as they want their bodies to resume the "normal" again.

When we have little or no strength, God is our refuge and strength, an ever present help in trouble. Trouble is distress. Grief is certainly distressful. God is ever present, always there. God is our strength. In the Hebrew "strength" ("*`oz*") is a "*defense, refuge, or protection, like a firm, secure fortified tower*" (Blue Letter Bible, "*`oz*"). Aren't those words comforting when you have no strength? Just picture God as a firm, secure fortified tower. Proverbs 18:10 says, "The name of the Lord is a strong tower; the righteous run to it and are safe." Perhaps you wonder if you have enough strength to even continue. Even one more day can feel like too much. Many just want to give up! This is so common.

When you have no more strength, it is the perfect storm, so to speak. It isn't the tornado, hurricane or earthquake storm. But it is the perfect storm for God to do His greatest work. I don't have to tell you that grief makes you about as weak as you can be. Paul says, "For when I am weak, then I am strong" (2 Corinthians 12:10). If you weren't so exhausted, you would certainly do whatever you could to make things right again. You would work hard to resume normal life. You would go back to your work and schedules, and you would try not to let the grief take over. You might even consciously push it to the back of your mind so you don't have to feel it.

Yet if you do all that, grief waits and it will come rushing back to you. Pushing it out of your mind will only work for so long. Grief has to have time to be processed. We have to "feel through it to heal." I often say, "As you are real, you feel, and you will heal." Even when you do this, you become exhausted and drained of your strength. So this is where you put yourself in the position to say, "Lord, I can't do this alone. Please help me!" And He will.

His perfect storm is to have you come to Him. He is able to console you. But you can't manipulate Him. You must wait upon Him, recognizing His timing is perfect. He lovingly seeks us to recognize that He is what we need.

When you are exhausted and deficient of strength, picture God as your defense, refuge, protection – that firm, secure fortified tower. Say, "Jesus." The name of the Lord is a strong tower. Picture yourself running to that strong tower for safety. Picture yourself closed up inside that tower of protection, safe from the storm of grief that would overtake you. Picture God filling you with His strength, while making you ready to go back out into the changing weather.

One more thing this passage says is that God is an ever-present help - "a very present help in trouble" (KJV). Here the Hebrew for "very" means *"very, exceedingly, greatly... emphatically doubled."* It also allows for *"quickly, hastily, which is also connected with the exertion of strength"* (Blue Letter Bible, *"m@`od"*). He is always able to strengthen you by the power of His Holy Spirit, but beyond that "very much, exceedingly, greatly," two times ever available to you to be your source of strength and "quickly, hastily!" You need encouragement like that! He's your strength in changing weather and He's a whisper away, willing quickly, exceedingly to be your refuge. Go to Him!

<u>Pray:</u> *Lord, I'm running to You. You are my strong tower. There is power in Your name. There is strength in Your name. No matter what the weather, You are my source of strength. Thank you, Lord. I grieve, I hurt, I'm exhausted. When I am weak, with no strength, You are a whisper away. How I praise You! Thank You for always being with me.*

CrossRoads for Thought:

- *When you are low on strength, what do you tend to do?*
- *Confess any actions you have taken in your grief that are not healthy. Let God remind you of His protection and love for you as His forgiveness washes over you.*
- *As you picture yourself entering God's tower of strength, sit in a quiet place and listen for His comfort and love for you.*

More Scriptures: Ps 28:7; Ps 59:17; Ps 61:3; Ps 118:14; Is 12:2; Is 25:4; Is 40:31; Phil 4:13

7. FAITH
–belief
(Also FAITHFULNESS)

<u>Hebrews 11:1</u> *Now faith is being sure of what we hope for and certain of what we do not see (NIV).*

*I*t hadn't been predicted! One hour I'm driving alone down the highway and the skies are partly cloudy. The next I'm caught in a heaven-opened deluge of rain. This unexpected seasonal torrential rain now consumes all my attention. I'm gripping the wheel tightly, white-knuckling it, straining with limited vision to just make out the edge of the white line on the road. At the same time my eyes are fixed on the barely visible tail lights of the cars ahead of me. My foot is positioned to move suddenly from the accelerator to the brakes in the event that anything ahead should quickly change.

Is it better to try to pull over and wait under an over-pass, hoping this weather will change? Or is trying to pull over going to cause an accident? Where are the rest stops? Exits? I can't see them...I can't see any signs, for that matter. I'm praying the entire time. I'm choosing to continue with many others surrounding me, as we slowly travel along doing the best we can to see through this driving rain. With heart racing, and all systems on alert, by faith I'm believing and trusting that eventually this weather will change with brighter skies down the road. It won't last forever, right? But I'm not to my destination yet. I have to survive this section of my journey and make it mile by mile, focused on what I'm doing and responsive to the actions of the cars traveling beside me.

Well, I made it! I had to! You've also navigated your car through the stormy seasonal rains. And I'm sure we will all go through more of them. Yet how like a grief journey is that seasonal torrential rain? For many, you are traveling through life and your journey is interrupted. You hadn't expected to lose someone you loved. And here you are, trying to navigate this unexpected storm <u>alone</u>. Where are the rest stops when the grief is pouring so hard? You can't see any signs for help! You are doing the best you can, along with others who are also traveling this road. But you are alone. You can't invite someone else to jump into the car and you say, "You take the wheel. I'm going to rest." You have to survive this journey. Day by day you continue, but you are getting more and more exhausted. Will it be this way forever? Will the grief weather change? Is there a final destination? If so, how close am I to it?

Good questions to ask. Just like the storms stop and blue skies await down the road, there are better days ahead on a grief journey. Granted, there are *both* harder and better days ahead. But your hardest work is surviving and not giving up the wheel of attention to making it through the grief. There is no rest stop which takes you off the journey. The hard work of going through it will pay off in a changed life for you. In fact, there can be new gifts recognized by working through the grief. Those may sound like hard words, but in the truest sense they are real. As you are going through the grief, God may be setting you up for some of His greatest work in your life.

It's all about faith...your having faith in God...faith in His faithfulness to all He has claimed He is and will be for you. Scripture says in Hebrews 11:1, "Now faith is being sure of what we hope for and certain of what we do not see." "Faith" in the Greek is *"pistis"* - *"a conviction of the truth of anything, belief"* (Blue Letter Bible, *"pistis"*). You hope for the unseen in a storm – eventually the weather will change. You have faith that change will happen in life as it does with weather.

Your faith in God is not rooted in weather systems. It is rooted in the character of God who has continually promised His faithfulness through His Word. Jesus is the living embodiment of God, the hope for your future. "And if Christ has not been raised, your faith is futile; you are still in your sins" (1 Corinthians 15:17). "But thanks be to God! He gives us the victory through our Lord Jesus Christ" (1 Corinthians 15:57). Our faith is based on the assurance that Jesus has paid our sin debt by His death. Every person who claimed to be God has a grave with the bones of a dead body, except Jesus! He rose from the dead. No bones to be seen at a gravesite! Instead, He showed Himself as the resurrected Lord for 40 days before ascending into heaven. Because He defeated sin, death, and the powers of hell, you will continue your journey of life and pass through death into heaven with Him.

As you navigate the journey of grief, God will show you new things along the way. Don't you see life differently? Isn't there a preciousness to life unlike you had before? You appreciate things now that you didn't appreciate in the past. You act differently. You learn more about compassion, as your life is touched both by those who do this well and those who do not do it well. These are just some of the varied gifts of grief that you accumulate along the way. Even your faith – the receiving of Jesus as your Savior – is a gift of grace. In fact, God says in Ephesians 2:8-9, "For it is by grace you have been saved, through faith – and this not from yourselves, it is the gift of God – not by works, so that no one can boast." You don't deserve faith. It is pure grace that God loved you and called you. He receives all the glory for saving you.

Now look at verse 10, "For we are His workmanship, created in Christ Jesus for good works, which God prepared beforehand so that we would walk in them" (New American Standard Bible). Do you realize that this continuing journey through grief is part of your life journey? God is not unaware that you are in this storm of life. He is preparing you for the good works He will do in and through you. You are His "workmanship." The Greek is *"poiēma"*- *"that which has been made; a work, of the works of God as creator"* (Blue Letter Bible, *"poiēma"*). "The Jerusalem Bible translates workmanship as 'work of art'" (Guzik "Ephesians 2"). You are His "work of art." You are His "masterpiece," on display for His glory.

You may feel like the last thing you are is a good witness for God. Instead, you may even wonder if God is there for you. How on earth could God be glorified through this tragedy? No one would wish this on a worst enemy. How could He have this be part of His plan for you? It's all about faith – faith and hope.

Faith in God who works in the unseen. Faith in God who has never broken one of His many promises. Faith in God who is well aware that your journey hurts. Faith in God who has an unseen place already prepared in heaven. Faith in God who can take the junk of your life, the grief, the hurts, the pains, and situations where you fail or lack faith, and turn them into beautiful gifts of testimonies to His faithfulness. He is the God of a Christian's faith. You are His work of art that is being transformed daily by the Sculptor's loving hands. Yield to Him that these often repeated phrases may be true: *Your mess becomes your message. Your test becomes your testimony. Your trial becomes your triumph.*

My journey through the torrential storm eventually took me to my final destination. This journey of life will continue on into heaven. You will continue to have other storms of grief on earth. The last will be the storm of death. What beauty of destination awaits you. Picture your life as His living "work of art," while changing along the way. When you see glimpses of the gifts of grief that He permits, you see His beauty coming through. It is way better than any earthly beauty that passes away. It's eternal! It's what others get to see as you are changed by His grace. I think we'll spend eternity seeing God's "works of art" in each other, and praising Him for His faithfulness in our lives.

Pray: Lord, You are the giver of faith. Increase my faith, please. I'm hanging on but I know I try to reason out this journey and it makes no sense. I can only cling to Your promises. You have never lied so I choose to trust Your ways and Your faithfulness. Are there really gifts of grief along the way? Yes! Help me to see them. I know you are sculpting me. It hurts! Please make my trial fit into Your triumph of the Cross. I can't make it beautiful but You can. Here I am!

CrossRoads for Thought:

- *Make a list of God's promises. Use your concordance or Google a listing. Read and meditate on this listing. Choose five promises. For each one, finish the sentence: God, as You promised to _____, You have been faithful in my life by _____.*

  (Example: Promise – Malachi 3:6: "I the Lord do not change."

  God, as You promised to <u>not change</u>, You have been faithful in my life by <u>not changing Your love to me, even when I have failed You</u>.)

- *Choose a Biblical character from the great chapter on faith in Hebrews 11. Look up the story. How did the mess become the message, the test become the testimony, the trial become the triumph? What probable emotions did the person experience along the way? How are you like that character? How did that one relate to God? How was that one faith-filled? How was God faithful? What did you learn?*

- *Do you have a saving faith in Jesus? If not, ask God for this gift. Confess your need for the Savior and ask Jesus into your life. Read Rom 3:23, Rom 6:23, Rom 10:13. Tell another Christian or a Pastor. Connect with a church to learn more about Jesus who loves you and what it means to follow and worship Him.*

<u>More Scriptures:</u> Ps 145:13; Rom 3:22-24; 1 Cor 10:13; Eph 6:16; Heb 10:23; 1 Pet 1:3-9

8. PEACE
   –of Christianity, the tranquil state of a soul assured of its salvation through Christ, and so fearing nothing from God and content with its earthly lot, of whatsoever sort that is

<u>Philippians 4:7</u> *And the peace of God, which passeth all understanding, shall keep your hearts and minds through Christ Jesus (KJV).*

*H*i! How are you? This expression happens every day all over the United States. It is our common greeting or salutation. After losing one we love, this common greeting often rings hollow. "Do you really want to know how I am? Do you really care? How much time do you have?" These questions we think, if not boldly ask at times. Most often the common words "OK" or "Fine" are murmured and are sufficient to cut off conversations, supplying the bare minimum of response needed to move on from those exchanges.

A common Jewish expression was and is the Hebrew word "Shalom." It means "Peace." Paul, who wrote most of the New Testament letters to the churches, used this powerful word in many of his greetings. He opened many letters with the words, "Grace and peace to you from God our Father and the Lord Jesus Christ" (Galatians 1:3). Some of the writings also include the added word mercy, thus "Grace, mercy and peace from God..." (2 Timothy 1:2).

So that we don't miss the power of these common words used together, let me give some brief definitions. First, grace is defined as unmerited worth. An acronym is GRACE – God's Riches At Christ's Expense. It is what God gives us, which as sinful people we *do not* deserve. Mercy is God's not giving us what we *do* deserve. Peace is what God gives to His people as a result of having His grace and mercy. It is a rest we have in Him that only comes through being justified by faith in Jesus. We can have peace with God because of Christ's atonement for our sins. They are forgiven because of Christ's death and resurrection.

For believers the challenge is living daily what we already positionally possess. It is living the life of sanctification – being set apart to do God's redemptive work. But we hurt and miss our loved ones. That doesn't feel peaceful at all.

Peace can feel like a fleeting emotion. Few, if any, would describe their grief as peaceful. Instead, many would say that this is an emotion they desire to feel again. The good news is that the Bible is packed with truths connected to this word "peace."

Paul says in Philippians 4:7, "And the peace of God, which passeth all understanding, shall keep your hearts and minds through Christ Jesus" (KJV). The Greek for "peace" (*"eirēnē"*) means *"of Christianity, the tranquil state of a soul assured of its salvation through Christ, and so fearing nothing from God and content with its earthly lot, of whatsoever sort that is"* (Blue Letter Bible, *"eirēnē"*). The key to understanding the peace of God comes from the verses both before and after. In Philippians 4:6 Paul tells the believer to go to God without being anxious over anything, but to take everything to God in prayer with thanksgiving. Then this peace of God, which passeth (surpasses) all human understanding, "shall keep" (*"phroureō")* means *"to protect by guarding"* (Blue Letter Bible, *"phroureō"*) your hearts and minds in Christ Jesus. Did you catch that? This peace of God surpasses all human understanding. No mere human can explain it. It only comes from God. It is His promise.

Next in Philippians 4:8-9, Paul says, "Finally, brothers and sisters, whatever is true, whatever is noble, whatever is right, whatever is pure, whatever is lovely, whatever is admirable – if anything is excellent or praiseworthy – think about such things. Whatever you have learned or received or heard from me, or seen in me – put it into practice. And the God of peace will be with you." In other words, "Think about such things. Do what I did. And the God of peace will be with you."

I see in Paul's words two principle steps to know the peace of God in your grief. First, be thankful. Paul is saying, "Pray to God about what is on your heart, but take it to God with thanksgiving." As I encourage the bereaved to be honest with God, that doesn't mean coating everything over with fake feelings. It means saying to God in all honesty, "Lord, I don't feel well. I am afraid. I hurt. I'm not sure

I can make it." But next is where these thoughts are transformed. "But Lord, You say that You will never leave me or forsake me. You say, 'Fear not, I have redeemed you.' Lord, I choose to believe that You will see my hurt and pain and make something good come from this. I don't know what it is but I choose to thank You for Your promises and Your faithfulness to me."

Can you see how taking the pain and giving it to God in thanks can bring peace? Speak thanks that is grounded in His character and nature. The enemy wants to keep you away from God and cause you to drown in fear, hurt, anxious thoughts and pain. Instead, run to God and find refuge under the shadow of His wings (Psalm 17:8; 91:4).

Second, daily take in God's Word; His truth is positive. Your mind dwells on what you put in it. Paul is saying that by thinking about all the good, you are controlling what you put into your mind. Your thoughts can be the playground of your flesh, sin and Satan. You can be your own worst enemy by what you hear, see, or read. You can and should protect your mind from what is in conflict with God's truth. It is one word – "SIN!" Be careful! You are vulnerable to many things as you grieve. You can rationalize and slip into patterns that contradict the safe place of truth in the Word. Satan will twist what you know and cause you to believe that new rules apply for you since you are in such a hurting state. Not true! When you put yourself in a position to sin and then rationalize your sin, you are removing yourself from the safety and security of the peace of God, which can guard your heart and mind in Christ.

Practice thinking and dwelling on the positive. Certainly you can speak what is negative to God, and perhaps to some safe people who won't misjudge you. That is being real. But then dwell on the positive and good. These are some practical ways to do this.

First, include it in your daily routine. Transform your mind *daily* in God's Word. Romans 12:2 says, "Do not conform any longer to the pattern of this world, but be transformed by the renewing of your mind. Then you will be able to test and approve what God's will is – his good, pleasing and perfect will." This powerful truth can change your mind and heart. 2 Corinthians 10:5 says, "We take captive every thought to make it obedient to Christ." When you are grieving, things that used to be normal and simple can become very challenging. This simple truth of being in God's Word is the most life-changing and life-giving thing you can do to find peace. The truth of the Word does bring peace into your heart and mind.

Second, surround yourself with like-minded people and put some distance between you and negative people. Determine the people who are not a healthy support for you and limit contact with them. You may need to construct some realistic boundaries. Find others in their grief who rely on their faith in the Lord. Connect with them to develop friendly relationships.

Third, continue your spiritual growth by connecting weekly with the body of Christ at a local church. Listen to God's Word being preached, spend time with fellow believers who can minister to you and pray with you, and receive assurance of God's grace, mercy and peace. If this was a part of your loved one's life with you, it will feel different. But trust that God will bring you to a deeper place in knowing Him as you work through the pain and find greater peace.

Last, be thankful. Dwell more on what is good. Examine your thought patterns. You may need to learn how to express your thoughts in a positive way.

Paul's words from the New Testament are still God's truth for today. May you know and experience "grace, mercy and peace from God the Father and Christ Jesus our Lord" (2 Timothy 1:2) as you go through your grief. Not only will you have the peace of God (Phil 4:7) but the God of peace will be with you (v. 9).

Pray: *Thank You for bringing me true and eternal peace through Jesus. Holy Spirit, I need the fruit of peace, which You give to believers, especially in times of grief. I want Your peace that is beyond human understanding. It only comes from You, Lord. I cannot find this peace on my own. I've tried many things that don't bring it. Forgive me, Lord, where I have tried to cover my pain and it has moved me away from You and Your Word. Forgive my sinful thoughts and deeds. Heal my mind and heart!*

CrossRoads for Thought:

- *Do you have peace with God through Jesus as your Savior? If not, and you want this peace, ask a Christian friend or a Pastor to pray with you for this ultimate peace.*
- *Do you lack peace in some area? Is God convicting you of sin to draw you back to repentance? If so, repent and let God's forgiveness shower your heart and mind with peace.*
- *Here are some suggestions for some practical steps to journey closer to finding some peace: Set up a daily Scripture reading schedule. Join a Christian support group. Set up a loving boundary with a negative friend. Join a church or participate weekly. Journal several things daily for which you are thankful. Examine what you read, see, and hear daily, and make changes needed to bring you peace.*

More Scriptures: Ps 29:11, Is 26:3; Jn 14:27; Rom 5:1; Gal 5:22; Col 3:15

9. SAD
–downcast; be despairing
(Also SADNESS)

<u>Psalm 43:5</u> *Why are you downcast, O my soul? Why so disturbed within me? Put your hope in God, for I will yet praise him, my Savior and my God (NIV).*

Alright, I admit it. I've done it, though very rarely. I bet you've done it too. You are reading along in a book and the drama is escalating. You are gripped with apprehension that the main character won't make the right choice and will mess up their life. You can't stand it! Your curiosity hits its limit and you do the unthinkable. You reticently turn to the last pages of the book, and you do what you know you shouldn't do. You know what I'm going to say…you read the ending!

Yes, I've done it. I say that with reluctance because once done, it changes the suspense and enjoyment of reading the book. It can spoil the fun of why you are reading it in the first place. From a different angle, you can sit back and enjoy the ups and downs of the story line, knowing that it is all going to end up alright (assuming it is a happy ending, that is).

Let's face it - the story line of life has its ups and downs. You can't go through life and not be affected by both joys and sorrows. You either die early in life, or you will walk through good and bad things. Not one person is exempt. You may have thought that life as a Christian would be easier. But we have God with us. It is true that He loves us and we have Jesus in us. Yet we remember His words in John 16:33, "In this world you will have trouble;" and John 15:20, "Remember the words I spoke to you: 'No servant is greater than his master.' If they persecuted me, they will persecute you also." Paul says in 2 Timothy 3:12, "In fact, everyone who wants to live a godly life in Christ Jesus will be persecuted." Bottom line – the Christian life is not free from troubles. You will have them if you are living a godly life. When you go through the hard stuff, there is no doubt it hurts. Whether the pain occurs as a result of just doing life, or whether it comes because you are walking in obedience to what God calls you to do, you are experiencing the broken picture of your dream. It is a "lost dream." When it involves the passing of someone that you love, you feel intense sadness as you inwardly (daily, hourly, minute-by-minute) process missing that person's presence. Many times you outwardly mourn. Webster's definition of sad is: *"affected with or expressive of grief or unhappiness; downcast"* (Def. "sad"). As the intensity deepens, the emotions can turn into depression. If so, the feelings do not subside or lift and you can barely function.

Psalms 42 and 43 provide words that aptly describe the sad heart of the bereaved. With honest words, the Psalmist lets you into the window of his soul as he calls out his lament to God. Here you find encouragement for those sad feelings. I love what the Psalmist repeats three times in Psalm 42:5-6; 42:11, 43:5. He says, "Why are you downcast, O my soul? Why so disturbed within me? Put your hope in God, for I will yet praise him, my Savior and my God." The Hebrew for "downcast" (*"shachach")* means *"be despairing"* (Blue Letter Bible, *"shachach"*).

Some days will be harder, and some days will be easier. Grief, and the process of going through it, can be similar to the waves of the ocean. It may feel like waves of grief that pour over your life for days. You can barely catch your breath. Then the waves go away until another time when they will pour over you again. The Psalmist aptly describes this distress in Psalm 42:7, "Deep calls to deep in the roar of your waterfalls; all your waves and breakers have swept over me." If you've ever been caught by a wave at the ocean and dragged under, you come out feeling bruised and beaten. If you aren't careful to move out of the way, you may have trouble with another wave. Grief is emotionally and physically exhausting. It can feel like those waves.

The Psalmist honestly laments with expressions like, "Why have you forgotten me" (Psalm 42:9)? "Why have you rejected me? Why must I go about mourning, oppressed by the enemy" (Psalm 43:2)? But please don't miss the gems of truth interspersed in this intense expression of distressed feelings. He says in Psalm 42:8, "By day the Lord directs his love, at night his song is with me – a prayer to the God of my life." Right in the center of his honest expressions of troubles, he notes that confession of hope. He is aware that no matter what he feels, God's love is still directing his life. At night he sings to his God, offering up a "prayer to the God of my life" (v. 8).

Can you see where *singing* and *prayer* can be tools of faith in the middle of your sadness? The entire book of Psalms is songs. They are written poetry or prayers put to music. What great examples God has given us to express ourselves to Him. While many of the Psalms are honest laments that express hurts, almost all end in praise to God. *Worship and praise form the ladder out of the pit of despair!* Scripture is filled with verses that refer to singing praise to God. It doesn't matter to God whether your singing voice is good or not. Ephesians 5:19 says, "Sing and make music in your heart to the Lord." Singing has a way of ushering you into God's presence when you need it most. You may sing with your own new song, singing out your prayer about how it hurts. As you are honest about the hurt, let your heart move to expressions of faith and praise as you recall God's character of love.

The truth in the three-time repeated refrain from these two Psalms is truly a gem. After asking himself why his soul is downcast and disturbed, the Psalmist makes an imperative statement to his soul. "Put your hope in God" (Psalm 42:5, 11: 43:5). It's like he is saying, "Soul, come on! Get your focus right!" In other words, "Soul, don't look at the hard things in life and dwell there, but instead look to your God, the God of HOPE, *MY* SAVIOR and *MY* GOD!" He has HOPE. His God is personal - my God! You can have that same HOPE. He is *your* Savior and God who has the victory over sin, death, and evil. There is a day coming when there will be no more sadness, no more pain, no more crying, no more death.

How do I know? I read the end of the book! And it's a great thing to do this time. You have the full truths of Scripture given for hope and encouragement. You don't have a blind faith. It is substantiated by facts and history. Our faith is based in the Savior, the God/man who lived for 33 years, died on the cross, and rose from the dead. Your final day of victory over sin, death, and the world is coming. Do you have that hope? Do you find comfort in knowing your loved one, if a believer in Jesus, is with God? No other one has done what Jesus did.

There may be a whole new book to read when we get to heaven. But I think it will take eternity to finish it. Guess I won't be jumping to the end of that book!

Pray: I have felt those waves of grief over and over. Some of them just wipe me out. I feel so overwhelmed with loss and sadness. Doing a minimum of daily functions can require too much energy. I'm so tired. My soul feels so ugly, dark, and empty on most days. I need Your Holy Spirit's help. I need hope! I know Your Word, and I know the end of the story. Help me to believe it and live it!

CrossRoads for Thought:

- *Look up more verses that talk about singing to God in a concordance or online resource. What new truths are you learning?*
- *Purposely plan times for music with some alone time. You may want to play traditional hymns or try new contemporary Christian songs. You can do this while at home, in the car, running, or exercising. Experiment by trying to make some of your own prayers and songs to God. Use the tools of prayer, writing, and singing to express yourself to God as a new means of worshiping Him. Try it regularly each week for a month to know how it helps.*
- *Are your times of sadness changing or fluctuating? If not, depression can require professional help. If necessary, seek professional help with a medical doctor or a counselor. This could be the most productive healthy step you can take. You should make an appointment just to be sure. It's OK to get help. Remember, Satan wants you stuck and drowning in your sadness. God gives hope and healing. Ask close friends and family for support and prayer.*

More Scriptures: Ps 59:16; Ps 108:1; Ps 130:5; Is 40:31; Jer 29:11; 2 Cor 7:6

10. ALONE
–separated from others; isolated

<u>1 Kings 19:14</u> *"I alone am left" (New King James Version).*

*A*lone! There are notable differences between aloneness, solitude and loneliness. Being alone is being
with no one else. Emotional feelings with aloneness can be
either positive or negative. Aloneness can be good, especially when chosen. Most of us like to be by ourselves at
times. Solitude is often a purposeful aloneness too, a good
chosen thing. In contrast, loneliness is associated with negative emotional feelings, ones not chosen and deeply felt.

In grief, emotional aloneness is most often felt as a
huge negative. It is a void that is isolating (Def. "alone"). A
bereaved person feels like no one else understands. The
pain and new journey of grief are intense and unpredictable. You can feel isolated from the closest of relatives and
friends. You can feel totally alone in a crowd of people. You
can even feel like God has left you in this mess of grief.

I love the story of Elijah found in 1 Kings 19. Take some
time to read about this prophet of God, but skim 1 Kings
18 first. He has just witnessed one of the most powerful
miracles of God. God revealed on Mount Carmel that He
alone is God. What a great spiritual victory. The God of
Israel is the only God. Immediately after that, Jezebel the
queen was infuriated and declared her quest to find Elijah
and kill him. Elijah became fearful and depressed by the

turn of events. He ran for his life and declared to God that he was tired and discouraged. He just wanted to die.

God, instead of granting his request, lovingly let him rest and provided food for him. He tenderly cared for His servant. After a journey of 40 days, God took Elijah to Mt. Horeb and gave him supernatural, powerful displays of His greatness. Later, in contrast to that, God spoke to His servant in a still, calm voice.

1 Kings 19:13-14 says, "So it was, when Elijah heard it, that he wrapped his face in his mantle and went out and stood in the entrance of the cave. Suddenly a voice came to him, and said, 'What are you doing here, Elijah?' And he said, 'I have been very zealous for the Lord God of hosts; because the children of Israel have forsaken your covenant, torn down your altars, and killed your prophets with the sword. I alone am left; and they seek to take my life'" (New King James Version).

Elijah heard God and told Him his situation and aloneness. Then God gave Elijah a new perspective and a task. It was to anoint a new king, Jehu, who would succeed the wicked King Ahab and his wife Jezebel. He was also to anoint a new prophet who would be a co-worker and friend. Then God told him he was not alone, and that there were 7000 others who obeyed God in Israel. That brought encouragement to the discouraged prophet who had felt alone. God was mightily at work way beyond his perspective and feelings.

How does this story apply to you in your grief? Consider these points:

1. It is clearly alright to be honest with God in your alone-ness. Elijah felt discouraged, depressed, and alone. He wanted to die. He cried out to God.

Many bereaved feel that kind of desperation after losing their loved ones. If you do, express them to God. He understands. He wants you to be honest and to trust Him. You love Him because He first loved you. But if you ever feel like you want to harm yourself or escape your feelings, get help immediately. Call someone you know and trust, or get professional help.

2. Elijah couldn't see beyond his present experience. He was aware that a vengeful Jezebel forced him to be a fugitive on the run. He felt alone. He went to God for direction.

You have feelings, which are real to you, but they are not the full picture. Trust God when you can't see what comes next. Go to Him through prayer and express your feelings. Then ask Him to help you see things from His perspective. Ask Him to give you what you need for each hour of everyday.

3. Though Elijah felt alone, he truly was never alone. God was always with him. There were also others he was unaware of who were obedient to God.

God helped him at his point of need. He gave him rest, food, and ministry by angels. He spoke to Elijah's heart in that gentle voice. He then revealed his next steps. He gave him a co-worker and others who were like-minded in following God. Notice this all took time. It didn't happen overnight.

God will do the same as you journey through your grief. You are never alone! He will tenderly meet you with what you need each day. You may need a season of good rest. Grief is difficult and exhausting, both emotionally and physically. (You may need to eat a better diet for your body to replenish needed nutrients). God is bigger than your grief and can reveal Himself to you in "that still small voice." Open the Word. Cry out to God. Let the Holy Spirit speak to you as you seek to hear God. It takes time!

Go to a church service or function to experience the body of Christ. Receive God's love and forgiveness through the ministry of others. Join a Bible study group. Connect with community grief support groups, or specifically a Christian support group (see today's CrossRoads for Thought for groups). You will find other Christians who can relate to the pain of loss by death. Establishing new relationships that are based on this common understanding of grief can be very healing. They can supplement the family, friend, and church support you may already have, and bring a new depth of caring.

4. God is at work in you through this life experience. Life's reality was far more than just the discouragement that Elijah saw. God helped Elijah see where he fit into God's Kingdom plans already in place. Elijah was not aware of the entire picture. He only had his perspective. He was aware that a vengeful Jezebel forced him to be a fugitive on the run. He felt alone and wanted to die. God had much more work for him to do. He had helpers ready and in

place. He gave him a heavenly perspective and new plans for his future.

Life's reality is always more than what you see. You only have an earthly perspective, but you can develop a heavenly perspective. Until God takes you to your heavenly home, you are here to do His work. He can take any deep life experience and use it for His Kingdom. Your name may not be Elijah, but God loves you the same and you are worth as much to Him as Elijah. He was an ordinary man. Read James 5:17. Do you trust that God is at work in your grief for His glory? He is!

Pray: I feel all alone at times. I find encouragement that Elijah felt alone too. Your Word says that he was a human just like me. I need to hear Your still quiet voice, Your gentle whisper. I want to trust Your plans whether You reveal them to me or not. I know You have a perspective that I can't see. Help me, Lord, today and all the days to come.

CrossRoads for Thought:

- *When do you feel most alone? What can you do to change the situation or environment to not feel as alone? Write down one action plan and do it. What is one healthy thing you like to do alone, but haven't done yet or recently? Make plans to do it.*
- *What is your personality? Are you an extrovert or an introvert? If you are more extroverted, purposely put yourself around others frequently so that you can interact. If you are more introverted, make plans to interact and get out with others. Avoid isolation. For a Christian grief support group, go to www.griefshare.org. This is a national organization with groups all over the country.*
- *You feel less alone when you move beyond your circumstances and do something for someone else. Think of someone going through a hard time and do something for that person.*

More Scriptures: Josh 1:5; Ps 62:1; 1 Tim 5:5; Heb 13:5-6

11. ANGER
–temper, wrath, indignation

<u>Ephesians 4:26-27</u> *"In your anger do not sin": Do not let the sun go down while you are still angry, and do not give the devil a foothold (NIV).*

You are traveling along, proceeding to enter the highway and you see it ahead – a traffic jam. There's no way off and no movement ahead. You are stuck. Grrrr! Not fun! Your first feeling to surface could be frustration or anger.

Just like a traffic jam you can enter a grief journey with the emotion of anger. And it can tie you up, making you feel "stuck." Let's consider a few thoughts that will help you deal with this strong emotion.

1. Sometimes anger is normal. It is a common emotion that we all feel at times; no one escapes it. It is not unique to grieving people. It is an emotion that you feel when you experience something that seems wrong. God gave you the ability to feel this emotion. Anger in and of itself is not sin. Scripture reveals God's anger. But His anger is always justified and holy. Human anger is easily caused by sinful behavior and pride. Do not think that you must always be in charge.

2. Many grieving people experience anger, especially in ways not typical for them. You are not alone in your anger.

But it may frighten you. Sometimes you don't even know with whom you are angry – no one and then everyone.

3. Anger must be dealt with in order to be healthy. Anger creates energy that must be released responsibly so that no harm is done to anyone. Anger uncontrolled can be harmful to yourself or to those you love. Anger should not be buried or stuffed inside. That creates both emotional and physical stress, leading to anxiety and depression. Anger turned inward often grows into bitterness, jealousy, rage, envy, or depression. Anger must be examined to find healthy and proper expression of its energy.

Why would a bereaved person feel angry? A partial list includes: people who don't understand what you are going through; well-intended words of comfort that don't comfort; illness; medical personnel; people who said they would call and they did not; loss of control; role changes within your family; couples or friends who are leaving you out of their social groups; the person who caused the reason for your anger; broken dreams; financial pressures; yourself or your loved one – for what was said or not said, or what was done or not done; and sometimes even God.

So how do you deal with the energy from anger? Do you "vent it out"? Do you diffuse it and calm it down? Remember, while God gave us the ability to feel this emotion, it can easily be tainted by sin and pride. You can justify anger at sin. The world is affected by sin. Perhaps your loved one was killed by a drunk driver. Or perhaps your loved one was abusive to you. Both situations could cause anger. But you do not want to express your anger in wrong ways. God is in charge. He is the one who executes His righteous judgment.

You may struggle in anger toward God because He allowed what caused your grief. Never forget that His permitting hurt in your life is coming from His love. If you are angry with God, go to Him. Tell Him. Read the Psalms. See how the Psalmist honestly expresses his anger, fear, and doubts. But in the process of going to God, his heart was changed and he was reminded that God was in charge.

If you want to retaliate, judge, and execute hurt with your anger, do not. God is patient, merciful, forgiving, loving, and redemptive. He never gives up on His children who are constantly messing up. Think about it – His anger at your sin hasn't been retaliation or punishment. Instead, it has been the riches of grace and mercy in sending Jesus to take your place. He took the full brunt of His anger toward your sin. He doesn't react to anger the way we do.

Ephesians 4:26-27 says, "Be angry, and yet do not sin; do not let the sun go down on your anger, and do not give the devil an opportunity" (NASB). The NIV says, "'In your anger do not sin': Do not let the sun go down while you are still angry, and do not give the devil a foothold." Be "angry" in the Greek is *("orgizō")* meaning *"to provoke, to arouse to anger"* (Blue Letter Bible, *"orgizō"*) and yet do not sin; do not let the sun go down on your "anger" *("parorgismos")* - *"indignation, exasperation"* (Blue Letter Bible, *"parorgismos"*); and do not give the devil an "opportunity" ("*topos*") - "*place, any portion or space marked off, as it were from surrounding space; power, occasion for acting*" (Blue Letter Bible, "*topos*").

You can have anger, but it is what you do with it that determines if it is sinful. If you do not give it over to God, you leave the door open to Satan and you continue to live in your grief and anger. Slam that door shut. I know it isn't easy, especially when the anger feels justified. But God will help you through it. Tell Him that you have harbored anger and you no longer want to be bound by it. By receiving God's forgiveness, you open yourself to His way and receive healing for your grief.

If you find it difficult to let go of your anger before the sun goes down, please consider the following:

1. Pray. Ask God to help you be in line with His heart. Ask Him if there is any action for good that He might want you to take based on righteous anger. Repent, confess, and receive forgiveness if you have nursed your anger and have expressed it inappropriately.

2. Remember, Satan desires to get a foothold in this area. Think about who the real enemy is (Ephesians 6:12), not the person with whom you are angry. Satan wants you to linger in anger. He wants you to yield to its control with bitterness, guilt, depression, judgment, retaliation, etc. Release this powerful emotion to God and take it back to Him as often as needed. Seek the Holy Spirit's help for direction.

3. Rest with God. Be willing to pray more as needed, for the situation or person. Leave this in His hands. If you find yourself slipping into rage, bitterness, guilt, retaliation, etc., remember, "'Vengeance is mine, I will repay,' says the Lord" (Romans 12:19, NKJV).

4. Remember, if God has forgiven you, how can you keep anger towards another? Recognize that God says, "Forgive, and you will be forgiven" (Luke 6:37). The Scripture says in Romans 12:18, "If it is possible, as far as it depends on you, live at peace with everyone." You can ask God to help your heart be right before Him in how you feel about others.

Pray: Lord, I need Your help to express my anger in a way that is not hurtful to others or myself. Even with You, Lord, sometimes I'm angry. Forgive me, Lord. I have not dealt with my anger in the right way. I have felt it and I have often expressed it in wrong ways. Sometimes I bury it; sometimes I fly off with it and hurt others; sometimes I'm so depressed and angry with myself. Thank You for Your love. Help me come to You as I am. It's too hard for me to control anger. I give myself to Your loving, merciful arms. Thank You, Lord, for Your forgiveness.

CrossRoads for Thought:

- *Experiment with healing ways to express your anger. Write down any angry thoughts you have in a notebook until you've exhausted every thought. Express your anger out loud in the privacy of your home. Pray your anger to God.*

- *What are some healthy ways you can discharge energy from anger? Experiment with exercise, walking, weeding, cleaning, punching a bag or pillow, or sports where you hit a ball. Start an organization or cause. Affect the political world. How can you make some things better?*

- *Is there anyone you have hurt with your anger? Is there anyone who has hurt you? The Scripture says, "If it is possible, as far as it depends on you, live at peace with everyone" (Romans 12:18). Ask for forgiveness when you have offended another. If you have been angered or hurt by someone, be willing to forgive them if the opportunity presents itself to do so. Ask God for His help with forgiveness, sometimes beginning with a confession of not even wanting to forgive. Prayer is incompatible with anger (1 Timothy 2:8). Remember in prayer and praise how deeply God has forgiven you. Let that be your motivation to forgive.*

More Scriptures: Ps 103:8-12; Ps 145:8; Mk 3:5; Rom 12:18-19; Col 3:8; James 1:19-20; 1 John 1:9

12. FEAR
–be afraid

Psalm 27:1 *The Lord is my light and my salvation – whom shall I fear? The Lord is the stronghold of my life – of whom shall I be afraid (NIV)?*

I'll get to the point of this one quickly and simply. When it comes to fear, <u>it's the difference between truths and lies.</u> That's it! Plain and simple.

If you are like me, your anxiety about the future tends to take over, especially in grief. There are many unknowns and "what ifs?" They can trap you in fear. They can be overpowering and you may wonder if you can even function, physically or mentally. What should you do?

First, let's think about visible situations. A poisonous snake within feet of you is a real fear. Fear of an approaching tornado that you can see is reality. With these types of fears, your body kicks in with the adrenaline needed and you act with a natural instinct for self-preservation. You do what you need to do for your protection.

Second, the fear you have with grief is not a fear that you see. It is one that you feel. It is fear about the future that takes place in your mind. It can begin with a real situation, and the thoughts about what "might" happen can take control. Some of this future thinking can be good if it prepares you to avoid problems. But too much of it causes you to dwell on the negative and to build strongholds of anxiety and fear that inhibit your functioning.

Consider the acronym FEAR – <u>F</u>alse <u>E</u>vidence <u>A</u>ppearing <u>R</u>eal. This is a valid description of those fears that trap you but are not based on reality; they only appear to be real. That is when the ability to discern between truth and lies becomes important for the Christian who is bereaved. When you are hurting and vulnerable, Satan can make your mind a playfield of doubt and fear. Things can appear real that aren't. I have an example to make this point.

I remember vividly a time when I was trapped by fear. I was scared about running into people I felt were unjust and in conflict with me. I became more anxious as my mind started thinking about what "might" happen. I read Psalm 27 and meditated on it. Try pausing and reading it now.

You see at the beginning that David the Psalmist wrote about a time of being afraid because his enemies were attacking. An army was besieging him; war was breaking out against him. Yet he says in Psalm 27:1, "The Lord is my light and my salvation – whom shall I fear? The Lord is the stronghold of my life – of whom shall I be afraid?" He declared in 27:5-6 that in the day of trouble God would keep him safe and hide him high upon a rock in the shelter of His tabernacle. His head would be exalted above the surrounding enemies while he would be shouting, singing, and praising God.

I meditated. In my mind I saw myself in this Scripture. I was high above my problems as I looked down at my enemies around me. I was safe with God as my stronghold.

My enemies couldn't see me because God had hidden me in His shelter. I was praising God and singing joyfully to Him with thanks. Were my problems real? Yes! Was my God greater? Yes! Was my God for me? Yes! He sheltered me as I was enveloped in joy and praise from being in His presence. My FEAR – false evidence appearing real – had been that I was surrounded and faced defeat. The reality was that God was with me. I was safe in His stronghold. My enemies were not robbing me of my joy. My vision was focused on Him and His truths.

On a grief journey there is a need to discern emotional fear by using the truth of God's Word. Look at 2 Corinthians 10:3-5. If you substitute fear as the thing you are waging war against (as well as anything Satan uses to trap you into negative strongholds) you then have a helpful passage that God has given to help discern truth from lies. It says you have God's power to demolish strongholds. That's what fear can become – a strangling stronghold. It can immobilize at times. The good news is that it can be demolished. How? Read verse 5. God says, "We demolish arguments and every pretension that sets itself up against the knowledge of God, and we take captive every thought to make it obedient to Christ."

It is saying that we "demolish" (*"kathaireō"*) - *"to refute"* (Blue Letter Bible, *"kathaireō"*) "arguments" (*"logismos"*) - *"a reasoning: such as is hostile to the Christian faith"* (Blue Letter Bible, *"logismos"*) and every "pretension" (*"hypsōma"*) - *"an elevated barrier"* (Blue Letter Bible, *"hypsōma"*) that sets itself up against the knowledge of

God and we "take captive" ("*aichmalōtizō*") - "*to subjugate, bring under control*" (Blue Letter Bible, "*aichmalōtizō*") every thought into "obedience" ("*hypakoē*") - "*obedience or submission of Christ's counsel*" (Blue Letter Bible, "*hypakoē*"). In other words, we refute reasonings that are hostile to the Christian faith. FEAR and all other barriers that set themselves up against God's truth must be taken captive under the submission of Christ's control. He will demolish them.

The truth is that God is your defender. He is your ever-present God, your stronghold and support when you are surrounded by fears and troubles. ANY argument, lie, or trouble you face that attempts to counter that truth is trumped and defeated as your mind brings it into submission to God's truth. He is with you, and no matter how severe the fear is or how horribly Satan attempts to batter you with worry, God is greater. Hallelujah! Fill your mind with God's truth and take every thought captive, making it obedient to the truth of God's Word.

You can say, "Fear, you have no room to stand in my life. You have been defeated at the cross and are under the submission of Christ. I say 'No' to fear in the name of Jesus." God's Word says (Psalm 56:3-4), "When I am afraid, I will trust in you. In God, whose word I praise, in God I trust; I will not be afraid." Speak this out loud. See it as putting down a faith marker. By doing this you are taking thoughts captive and making them obedient to Christ. Trust that God will work as you renounce sin and its power over you; and draw near to God in trust that He loves you and will shelter you. The Scripture from 2 Corinthians 10:3-5 is a life-long tool of defense to wield in defeating lies that come against you in your faith walk, especially in defeating fear in your life.

Are fears hard? Yes! Can they be under God's submission? Yes! Are your fears important to God? Yes! Is He your ever-present stronghold and refuge for fear? Yes! Satan's strongholds demolished? Yes! God's stronghold established? Yes! Is this all truth? Yes, and amen!

Pray: I know You care about my fears, Lord. Sometimes my mind races with worry and concern about the future and decisions that I need to make now. Help me take my thoughts and submit them to You, Lord. Enable me to stand on the truth that You love me. I can face anything with Your help. Let me trust You to guide me with each step. Keep Satan and his lies far from me. Send Your angels to watch over and protect me.

CrossRoads for Thought:

- *When are you most fearful? Note if there are times of the day, occasions, or people that affect this. Have faith markers and write down what they are. Speak truth out loud over these times or situations. If you're overwhelmed with fear, speak the name of Jesus. If you find yourself stuck in fear, ask for help from a minister, counselor, or doctor. God can use these professionals to help you in the hardest of times. It can be your healthiest step.*
- *Make a fear and worry chart with two columns and put today's date on it. Write every fear and worry down that you have on separate lines. When finished, pray that God will make a way with each one. Put the chart away and bring it out in three months. How many of your fears were false? How many fears did God take care of for you? Use this tool to help you build faith and trust in God.*
- *Scripture is filled with verses to counteract fear and find truth. Continue by using a concordance to study "fear" and "stronghold." Memorize any Scripture verse that is most helpful to you.*

More Scriptures: Ps 23:4; Psalm 27; Psalm 56; Psalm 91; Is 41:10; Nah 1:7; 2 Cor 10:3-5

13. SORROW
–grief, anguish

<u>Jeremiah 8:18</u> "*O my Comforter in sorrow, my heart is faint within me*" *(NIV).*

wo of them, reaching out – you see them and there is no mistake. Two hands – reaching straight out in front with palms up, or reaching up in the air. I've experienced it with each of my children. I've seen it in foreign countries from starving children. How effective extended hands, palms out or up, can be! It's hard to pass them by.

I love how God packed His Word with so many treasures. Just as your suitcase must be carefully packed with what you will need for a journey, God has packed His Word with everything you will need for the journey of life. The Ten Commandments, Jesus' words in the New Testament, and all the inspired writings of the patriarchs, prophets, and apostles, are filled with relevant truths. There is encouragement no matter what you experience in life. Within its pages the Holy Spirit can bring God's truth and intimate love into your life. Words that you may have read before and hardly noticed can bring exactly what is needed.

In the verse from Jeremiah, the prophet is identifying his love for his people (Judah) who have fallen away from God. He was proclaiming the coming judgment of exile to Babylon, if the people did not repent. This weeping prophet's words fell on deaf ears. His love for the people was evident by the deep sorrow he felt. In Jeremiah 8:18 he exclaims to God, "O my Comforter in sorrow, my heart is faint within me." His "sorrow" (*"yagown"*) meaning *"grief, anguish"* (Blue Letter Bible, *"yagown"*) was so deep that it had physical and emotional effects. "Since my people are crushed, I am crushed; I mourn, and horror grips me" (Jeremiah 8:21).

Webster's definition of mourning is "an outward sign of grief for a person's death" (Def. "mourning"). Mourning is what comes out, what others see expressed. Two examples are tears and anger. What is outwardly expressed constitutes what we call mourning.

Here's where God's suitcase for life, the Word, is packed with examples. Read Psalm 6:6 and Psalm 38:9-10. They describe "mourning" (*"'anachah"*) meaning *"sighing, groaning (expression of grief or physical distress)"* (Blue Letter Bible, *"'anachah")* with words like "worn out from groaning; flood my bed with weeping; drench my couch with tears; eyes grow weak with sorrow; heart pounds; my strength fails me; the light has gone from my eyes." Psalm 88:9 says, "My eyes are dim with grief." Have you had drenched pillows, heart racing episodes, or puffy bags under your eyes? If so, you can relate. On a hard grief day, can't you insert your name in front of each of these clauses and identify with them? Like each of them, you have some days where you intensely feel the sorrow which is expressed by mourning.

How do you find a way to navigate this intense sorrow? No one wants to walk through pain. You will not heal if you try to avoid it or go around it. Find times to engage the grief and move toward it, not away from it. As God takes you through the pain and you allow its outward expression in mourning, you will begin to find your healing path. What it looks like from person to person will vary. That's alright. We all have different personalities so you may not grieve the same as another person. The principle here is to move through it rather than trying to avoid it. There will be times when you purposely do other things so you don't feel it all the time. That is natural and healthy. Just make sure you don't hide from the grief, thinking time will make it better. It usually doesn't. It's your willingness to go through it that will help.

Here is where God's Word gives us another helpful insight. Psalm 88:9 says, "My eyes are dim with grief. I call to you, O Lord, every day; I spread out my hands to you." The key question here is: "In relation to my grief today, what is my position?" Are you angry at God and turned away from Him? Or are you angry with God and turned toward Him? Have you moved away from Him and your faith because He took your loved one away? Or are you looking up to God with tears rolling down your face? Are you asking for His understanding as you admit you are stuck with questions about His love?

What is the position of your hands, your fingers? Are they balled in fists clenched with anger and pain? Are they pointing in frustration and blame toward someone or God? Are they laid out in front of you opened and waiting for answers? Or are they extended above you as you call out in agony for help?

Go to God in honesty and humility if you want to find healing. Only He has all the answers. He has love for you. He can do His most beautiful work in you through the pain. Because of Jesus you can know His blessings. He gave you others to love – family, friends, etc. If your pain is from the loss of one you loved, to have known that love was God's gift to you.

Any grief you work through is God's opportunity to refine you and to change your heart to be more like His. But what happens will depend on your position - the position of your heart, the position of your hands. As the clenched fists become unrolled, the pointing fingers dropped, the palms turned open, and the hands stretched upwards, you position yourself in humility to receive far more than you could ever imagine. As the palms extend upward, the tears rolling down, the heart opens up to worship and praise of God whose ways are not our ways. "As the heavens are higher than the earth, so are my ways higher than your ways and my thoughts than your thoughts" (Isaiah 55:9). He knows what He is doing. "He guides the humble in what is right and teaches them his way. All the ways of the Lord are loving and faithful for those who keep the demands of his covenant" (Psalm 25:9-10).

My soul is touched deeply by the extended hands of a little one or aging weathered hands. I can't help but react. What about God? Do your extended hands in desperation matter to Him? He is bound by His love for you. Position yourself for Him to do His greatest work in you.

Pray: I am often beaten down in my sorrow with little energy to function. Some days my attitude stinks and I barely care. I know I can't do this on my own. Help me desire to be in a position to receive Your help. I thought I knew what was best but I'm slowly realizing You have a better plan. I liked my old plan. Help! My hands are up. I know You see me.

CrossRoads for Thought:

- *Do you have a place in your home where you go to God regularly? Equip it with what you need to help you connect to God, e.g., chair, pillow, Kleenex, pen, paper, Bible, candle, music, etc. Make it a place to seek and honor God.*

- *Physical position can open the heart to receive. Experiment with different positions of humility to receive from God. One method is to sit still, quieting your spirit and mind. Pray to God what is on your heart. Then move your palms up on your lap, sitting quietly, asking God to fill your mind with what His Spirit will tell you. You can experiment with the palms open and up position. If you are physically able, try sitting, standing with arms up, kneeling, or lying prostrate on the floor.*

- *Set up a "mourning time" with a safe friend. Before you start, ask the friend to just listen for awhile. Allow yourself to express your sorrow outwardly in this safe way. If your friend is another bereaved person, you may want to take turns. Decide in advance you will go for ice cream, coffee, or whatever activity the two of you want when this time is done.*

More Scriptures: Job 17:7; Ps 31:10; Ps 46:10; Is 35:10; Is 51:11; Eph 4:2; 1 Pet 5:6-7

14. TEARS
– an expression of weeping and grieving

<u>Psalm 56:8</u> *Record my lament; list my tears on your scroll – are they not in your record (NIV)?*

It's funny how sounds stick with us. I can still remember that high-pitched, shrill sound of my mom's pressure cooker as we were canning fruits and vegetables. While that heavy pot didn't look scary, it certainly was to me. I didn't understand it but my mom did, especially that pressure release valve on top of the pressure cooker. That little valve made a world of difference as the heated up molecules of water began expanding and taking up more volume. As heat changed the water from liquid to vapor, that valve allowed for the escape of the increasing pressure. If not, the lid would literally blow off the cooker. No one wants an explosion in the kitchen! That pressure cooker demanded respect. It certainly helped to understand the importance of that release valve.

That pot reminds me of tears. The big cooker needed its release valve in order to work properly. You have a "release valve" too. Tears are a relief – a result of our safety "release valve" working properly. God in His infinite wisdom made that for your survival.

Emotional extremes – joyful happiness as well as deep sadness and mourning can cause tears to flow. What a gift God has given you. Some emotions are too much to contain. How sad that some have been raised to believe that they should not release tears. Some have been conditioned to believe that tears should be denied, dreaded, feared, or hated. But they flow from your safety "release valve" as the "pressure cooker" of life builds up with lots of emotional stuff. You can release it. You need the relief, <u>especially</u> on a grief journey.

How do you feel about tears? The point here is not how much or how often you cry. The point is: *If you need to cry, it is OK.* It's that simple. That's why you have the safety valve for your emotions and feelings. God knew what you would need to survive. As long as you have not been influenced negatively about the importance of your feelings, you will naturally cry and feel what you need to feel when you need to feel it.

You may have been told by family members or others not to cry and that crying is a sign of weakness. You should "pull yourself up by your boot straps and get over this. Be strong!" Wrong! Since when have denial, anger, and stuffing feelings become healthier than allowing honest expressions of hurt and pain? It may feel strange at first. But it makes perfect sense. You are like that pressure cooker. You need to express emotions in healthy ways. That "strong" bereaved person is one who knows or learns the need to process through feelings and pain to heal.

Tears are your friends and not your enemies. But they can come when you don't want them or expect them. Then they don't stop. Grief is very slippery and can't be totally managed. This can be frustrating for people who like to control their situations. You probably are recognizing that grief is unlike anything you've ever experienced. You can educate yourself about grief but you can't totally predict it or plan it. Avoiding the grief or tears won't help. You must allow yourself to go through them, just like the pressure cooker. Do you realize that if the tears go "out," then the stress is not going "in"? It is being processed "out" of your body, which brings healing. Stress can cause various health problems. Remember to give yourself permission to cry when you need to cry.

I love the examples in God's Word that support this outlet for grief. It uses various words for tears, weeping, wept, and crying. One Hebrew word, *"bakah,"* meaning *"to weep (in grief, humiliation, or joy) bewail, cry, shed tears"* (Blue Letter Bible, *"bakah"*) is used numerous times throughout the Old Testament to describe the weeping that accompanies both grief and joy. We see Jacob weep (*"bakah"*) with joy in Genesis 29:11 when he meets his future wife Rachel. Later we see Jacob weep and mourn (*"bakah")* with grief (Genesis 37:35) when he believed that his son Joseph had died.

We see several instances of Jesus weeping or crying. As He was preparing to go the cross, He stopped and looked over Jerusalem, the city of His beloved people. Luke 19:41 says, "As he approached Jerusalem and saw the city, he wept over it." He was grieving because the people for whom He came did not understand the type of kingdom He represented. That beloved city would be given over to death, destruction, and pain after His death and resurrection. He wept for it.

Another instance of Jesus' crying is recorded in John 11:35. Many know it as the shortest verse in the Bible: "Jesus wept." The Greek here is the word *"dakryō" – "to weep, shed tears"* (Blue Letter Bible, *"dakryō"*). It is the only time this word is used in the New Testament and it describes Jesus' tears over the death of His friend Lazarus. Jesus was moved to tears as He saw Mary and Martha with their grief. Such compassion He felt for that family.

While grief is expressed with other terms in Scripture, one of the most intriguing references to tears is found in Psalm 56:8, "Thou tellest my wanderings: put thou my tears into thy bottle: [are they] not in thy book" (KJV)? The NIV is, "Record my lament; list my tears on your scroll – are they not in your record?" The New Living Translation is, "You keep track of all my sorrows. You have collected all my tears in your bottle. You have recorded each one in your book." In explaining what is meant in this verse, Jamieson, Fausset, and Brown write about David, "God is mindful of his exile and remembers his tears. The custom of *bottling the tears* of mourners as a memorial, which has existed in some Eastern nations, may explain the figure" (Jamieson, Fausset, and Brown "Commentary on Psalm 56"). This explanation allows for God to catch each tear that falls, tenderly aware of the grief.

How comforting to know that your God cares so intimately about your life, your hurts, pain, and grief. Not one is missed by your loving God! When you hurt and feel the need to cry, use the release valve God gave your body. Unlike the whistling pressure cooker, God catches the tears that you release. He comforts you and walks with you through the grief. There is nothing He can't redeem and use for your good and His Kingdom purposes.

Pray: *O Lord, sometimes I wonder how many bottles I have filled with tears. I haven't liked tears as I hurt so much when I cry. Help me to see them as Your gift for me to express my pain and hurt, especially to You. I'm glad You understand my grief, Lord.*

CrossRoads for Thought:

- *What did you learn about tears from your family or society? Is it truth? What does God say about tears? How does this impact your grief expression?*
- *Times of tears can release stress. Look at pictures of your loved one, put on music, and set the surroundings to help you feel your grief. Allow yourself to cry as long as you need. If you have difficulty being able to cry, set a timer and allow yourself to feel whatever you feel for 20 minutes. At the end of the time get up and do something else. Continue this process until you feel like your tears are more manageable.*
- *Find a "safe person" that you can talk with and express your emotions. Set up a time to meet in a safe place to talk about your loved one and cry if needed. Trust your friend to care without stopping the expression of tears.*

More Scriptures: 2 Ki 20:5; Ps 6:6; Ps 116:8; Ps 126:5; Ecc 3:4; Is 25:8; Heb 5:7; Rev 21:4

15. ABANDON
–desert, leave in straits, leave helpless (Also ABANDONMENT, ABANDONED)

<u>Hebrews 13:5</u> *"Never will I leave you; never will I forsake you" (NIV).*

I can remember it like yesterday! Having walked through difficult times, the memories connected with those times can be emotionally retrieved quickly. One of the worst times in my life did not last long. But it certainly didn't feel like it at the time. Things were chaotic around me and all my support systems I normally had either didn't feel totally safe or they were confused too. I felt all alone – a new feeling I had never had. So I waited for God to help me. I was talking to Him all the time. I dug deeper into His Word. I continued my journaling. I was waiting for God to speak to me and give me encouragement and hope.

I expected God to speak through Scripture. That had always been the way He had revealed Himself to me. But as I read the Word, it seemed dry. I was becoming more desperate. I needed to hear His comfort, direction and encouragement. I read, I prayed, I waited but I received nothing. Why wasn't He speaking to me? I had no answer.

I was getting frustrated with God. Feeling deserted by Him, I struggled with what to do. Where else could I turn? I had no other reliable source. I journaled my frustration. I needed Him now more than ever. As I continued to read the Word daily, I questioned my own faith. Where was God? I had no answers. He had abandoned me; that is how I felt.

The reality is that God was there. He had never abandoned me. I questioned Him. I complained. Yet when He spoke, He caught my attention like never before. He helped me examine my faith and to trust Him when He didn't do things on my timetable. Would I continue to believe and come to Him when His ways didn't make sense to me? Would I believe He was there, loving and working on my behalf, when He appeared to do the opposite? Would I trust Him during hard times, when they didn't end quickly or well?

When death occurs a bereaved person can feel totally alone, like no one else understands. If God is questioned, a sense of abandonment can be overwhelming. It is a desperate place to be. But consider the truth in this verse, "Never will I leave you; never will I forsake you" (Hebrews 13:5). The Greek word "forsake" (*"egkataleipō"*) meaning *"abandon, desert, leave in straits, leave helpless"* (Blue Letter Bible, *"egkataleipō"*) is close to the English word "abandon." These words are spoken by God to His people. Notice the word "never" repeated. Spurgeon is quoted, "You that are familiar with the Greek text know that there are five negatives here. Here the negatives have a fivefold force. It is as though it said, 'I will not, not leave thee; I will never, no never, forsake thee.' " (Guzik, "Hebrews 13"). I can picture our Lord saying five times over, "Never, Never, Never, Never, Never will I leave you nor forsake you."

Be sure you note the whole of Scripture. The Bible gives a picture of God as complex. He is loving, yet just. He is full of grace, yet punishes sin. He is merciful, yet just. He saves some, yet condemns others to hell. Nevertheless, the big picture reveals Him as loving, gracious, and merciful.

Jesus says in Matthew 27:46, "My God, my God, why have you forsaken me?" The word "forsaken" (*"egkataleipō"*) meaning *"abandon, desert, leave in straits, leave helpless"* (Blue Letter Bible, *"egkataleipō"*) speaks of our Savior Jesus who became sin in our place. Our punishment was laid upon Jesus. He bore the abandonment of His Father for us. God made the way for us by sacrificing His own dear Son. Through His death on the cross where He was "forsaken" by His Father, believers are now the Father's redeemed children. We will never be forsaken or abandoned by God. Jesus experienced that for us.

So when you have those fleeting or lasting feelings of being abandoned, they do not portray the truth. You are never alone! God is always with you. Jesus, being both God and man, understands how it feels to be abandoned in a way you will never know. He hears you when you are hurting or crying. Sometimes it feels like God "hides" Himself for a season, but He is there and will reveal Himself to you in the way that is best for you.

Hebrews 11:1 says, "Now faith is being sure of what we hope for and certain of what we do not see." When I couldn't "see" God's working in my life, I clung to my faith. I kept praying, reading God's Word, and going to Him with honesty in my frustration and aloneness. It was a foggy, confusing time for me.

Grief is the same way. It is foggy, confusing, and possibly the most challenging season you will ever experience. By faith go to God through Jesus in prayer. He can handle you as you are. He's there when you can't see Him. Trust this truth, "Never will I leave you; never will I forsake you." You may not see it at the moment. But it is the truth!

Pray: Are you really there, Lord? Do You really care? I feel alone, let down by family and friends. I feel like no one knows the depth of my pain. I'm talking to You. I'm calling out to You, Lord. I'm desperate to know You really do love me. Please, God, if You loved me enough to send Your Son to take my place, help me to cling to that and believe Your promise never to abandon me. O Lord, please help me.

CrossRoads for Thought:

- *Jesus was abandoned so you never will have to experience that. He knows your thoughts. As your mediator and High Priest, He prays for you in heaven. Put a chair across from you and picture Jesus there. What will you say to Him? Listen in quiet. What would He say back to you?*

- *Light chases away darkness. God's Word is the Light and Truth. Write Scripture verses on note cards or Post-it notes. Put them where you can see them and use them when you doubt or when darkness starts to overwhelm you. Light and darkness cannot coexist.*

- *When feeling abandoned, you need the body of Christ for support. It's a step of trust. You also need your church regularly in order to hear the Truth and to experience God's love and forgiveness through Holy Communion. Talk to someone there for encouragement, prayer, or confidential support. Recognize that one day you may be able to do this for someone else.*

More Scriptures: Deut 4:31; Ps 71:9; Is 42:16; Acts 2:31-33; Rom 8:34; 2 Cor 4:9; Heb 7:25

16. DESPAIR
–to be utterly at loss, be utterly destitute of measures or resources, to renounce all hope

2 Corinthians 4:8-9 *We are hard pressed on every side, but not crushed; perplexed, but not in despair; persecuted, but not abandoned; struck down, but not destroyed (NIV).*

*M*any people will be able to relate to this subject – losing weight! We tend to put on more weight as we age. There are exceptions, but this is a problem for a lot of people. The pounds are gradually added. We are blessed with the type, quantity and quality of foods to enjoy.

You may know the roller-coaster effects of gaining and losing weight. It is frustrating. Exercising and losing weight gets harder as time passes. Eating that five course meal feels so good going down, but it can lead to despair when the weight on the scale creeps higher.

If you are recently bereaved you may notice a change with your eating. It is not abnormal to have sudden vacillation with weight. Some express that there is no appetite whatsoever. Food has no attraction at all and they have to force themselves to eat. Weight loss can occur very rapidly with the crisis of grief.

The opposite also can occur. A person can turn to food as a comfort. Fast food can give some immediate pleasure, but this "adds" to the problem of grief. Excess weight is gained and the grief still exists. The quick fix can add despair on top of the existing pain.

Paul talked about hard times as he preached the gospel message. In 2 Corinthians 4:7, he mentioned having the treasure of the gospel in "jars of clay." This means that the good news of God's love comes through frail humans. God gets all the glory. Then Paul talked about the opposite. He said, "We are hard pressed, but not crushed; perplexed, but not in despair; persecuted but not abandoned; struck down, but not destroyed" (2 Corinthians 4:8-9).

To learn more about Paul's challenging life, read 2 Corinthians 11:23-29. Be encouraged by Paul's honesty, then relate that to the challenging times in your life. Having a loved one die can be the hardest thing that you will ever endure. But you can be encouraged to defeat the despair of life.

"Despair" – "*exaporeō*" in the Greek (verse 8) means *"to be utterly at loss, be utterly destitute of measures or resources, to renounce all hope"* (Blue Letter Bible, *"exaporeō"*). There is good news. If you are reading this, you are still pursuing hope. You haven't given up. God has more good news for you.

Paul said he was "perplexed, but not in despair." "Perplexed" ("*aporeō*" in the Greek) means *"to be at a loss with one's self, be in doubt; not to know how to decide or what to do"* (Blue Letter Bible, *"aporeō"*). If this doesn't describe normal grief, I don't know what does. You may be perplexed by your new situation. You may not know what to do and even doubt many things that you never doubted before. That could even include God.

Paul endured many situations that could cause feelings of despair and hopelessness. Why could he say he was perplexed but NOT in despair? If you read the rest of the chapter, you will find the answer. He talks about revealing Christ through our bodies (lives) so that grace is spread and God is glorified (2 Corinthians 4:10-15). It's about God being glorified in all that we do.

Note especially verses 16-18. We don't lose heart and give up in despair. We are wasting away outwardly, but inwardly God renews us day by day. "For our light and momentary troubles are achieving for us an eternal glory that far outweighs them all" (v. 17). Let's see how this relates to grieving.

First, it clearly does NOT mean we gain salvation by what we do. Salvation comes through faith alone in Jesus Christ and what His life and death accomplished for all who believe in Him. This means any troubles that you endure are opportunities for Him to be glorified. It's not about you; it's about God. Your grief and perplexity over events of life can be used by Him to point others to your source of hope. He is the only source of hope. His work in you ministers to others. They see that your faith makes a difference. Even if you struggle with God, you at least go to Him.

Second, grief does not seem light and momentary. It is deep and lonely. God can use this trouble to help others see Him in you. When compared to eternity, it is momentary and light. You are different because you have a real

God you can talk to, pray to, wrestle with; who cares about you and loves you no matter what. You have a different answer to the perplexity of grief. And God gets all the glory.

The King James Version (2 Corinthians 4:17) says, "For our light affliction, which is but for a moment, worketh for us a far more exceeding and eternal weight of glory." Think ahead. This is a picture of our future. Jamieson, Fausset, and Brown say, "'The lightness of affliction' contrasts beautifully with the 'weight of the glory'" (Jamieson, Fausset, and Brown "Commentary on 2 Corinthians 4:17"). The "weight" ("*baros*" in the Greek) is *"a weight of glory never to cease, vast and transcended glory"* (Blue Letter Bible, "baros"). The "glory" ("*doxa*" in the Greek) is *"the glorious condition of blessedness into which is appointed and promised that true Christians shall enter after their Saviour's return from heaven"* (Blue Letter Bible, *"doxa"*). The unseen is eternal; it is a state of blessedness. It is vast and transcendent, beyond our imagination. Those who die in Christ see Him in a way we have yet to experience. This world and all it holds will not compare to the treasure and glory of the next. This is good news that fights despair. The weight of glory wins out over the light, momentary affliction. Hallelujah! Wow!

Overeating with weight gain is not good. Losing weight rapidly due to stress is not good. But the weight gain of glory that is yet to come cannot compare with the trials of this life. Thank God that there is an answer for despair and it lies in knowing that there is a greater glory beyond this life. Don't lose heart. Go to Him and have Him renew you day by day in His Word with love and comfort. I look forward to joining you and seeing your "glory weight" in heaven.

Pray: Lord, sometimes I hurt and I have doubts. I've almost lost hope. Help me fight despair and not lose heart. Help me see beyond this life to the unseen and beyond this temporary pain to the glory of the next. Your Word says You have not abandoned me. You will renew me day by day. Holy Spirit, please minister Your comfort to me. As You strengthen me, may Your life be revealed through me to those who need You. Even in my pain, I desire You to be glorified in me.

CrossRoads for Thought:

- *When you despair think of a "safe person" that you can turn to for prayer. Ask if they can pray with you.*
- *If you are having a hard time turning to God, recognize the weight of despair is heavy. Seek professional help if you despair of life. The enemy Satan speaks lies about God to discourage. There is power in the name of Jesus. Just saying His name brings hope. Keep saying His name and get the professional help or prayer that is needed.*
- *Can you even imagine the glory yet to come? Spend time thanking God for His mercy and grace that covers you. You will see this glorious God someday. Thanksgiving brings hope!*

More Scriptures: Jn 14:18; Rom 5:3-5; Rom 8:35; 1 Cor 10:13; Heb 13:5

17. LOST
–to lose oneself, to wander

<u>Psalm 119:176</u> *I have strayed like a lost sheep. Seek your servant, for I have not forgotten your commands (NIV).*

We've all had those moments. They seem incredibly long but often are just seconds. Terror and panic cross our minds. You fill in your own life experience... it's the moment when you realize your credit card is not in your wallet; it's the split second when you don't see your parents at the amusement park; you turn back and don't see your toddler in a busy place. What do you do next? In all of these situations, you've either lost something or someone. When the lost is found and the anxiety and panic flee, relief rushes in like a huge wave.

Before the days of GPS my husband and I were traveling from Michigan to the south to move into our new home. We had been married for only three months. All our belongings were in two vehicles – our car and a U-Haul rental truck. Since I had mapped out our route, I drove the car in front and my husband was behind with a friend in the U-Haul truck. While going around Chicago, the weather turned into torrential rain and traffic separated our caravan of two. I took the exit as planned. In my rearview mirror, I saw them pass the intended exit. Oh no! Panic! Now what to do? No cell phones. Would they turn around and see the right exit? What should I do? All kinds of questions but no answers.

We had about an eight hour drive remaining to our new home and I was scared. As tears streamed down my face, I prayed that the Lord would get us there safely, even if I did not see them along the way.

The Word has a lot to say about being lost. In Psalm 119 the Psalmist focuses on God's Word in two directions. One is on living a life of obedience. The other is relying on faith. There are lots of promises of God mixed in with practical life directives. In Psalm 119:176 the Psalmist says, "I have strayed like a lost sheep." The Hebrew for lost ("*'abad'*") means *"to be lost, to lose oneself, to wander, of a lost and wandering sheep"* (Blue Letter Bible, *"abad"*). It is common for the bereaved to feel "lost." Life is not the same. YOU aren't the same. Others act differently towards you. There is a fog that is heavy at the beginning. Later the fog may lift and the reality of the loss of your deceased is felt in different ways. Where is the happy self you used to be? Where is the desire for things you liked before? You feel lost.

Even your once solid foundation of faith can feel lost. You used to pray, to be with your church, to read the Word, but now you can't. You try but you feel numb. Even to cry out to God feels fake. Is He even there? It feels like He is not. You may question if God even exists.

Why are Christians compared to sheep in the Scriptures? Perhaps it is because it provides a perfect analogy for how we act alike. Sheep are focused on themselves and they are prone to wander. As sheep tend to wander from their shepherds, we by nature are prone to wander from our loving God into unknown areas of harm, better known as sin. I like what Matthew Henry shares. He says, "We are apt to wander like sheep, and very unapt, when we have gone astray, to find the way again. By going astray we lose the comfort of the green pastures and expose ourselves to a thousand mischiefs" (Henry, "Commentary on Psalm 119:176").

What is hard about grief is that you don't intentionally desire to be lost or to wander from God. It happens due to the intense pain of the loss. You hurt and are overwhelmed beyond your understanding. It's like the torrential rain I described and it is hard to see your way. You may lose sight of your Master Shepherd and begin to listen to the lies of the enemy who would have you feel lost, discouraged, and hopeless. Remember, Satan is the master of lies. He distorts the truth.

The Psalmist says, "Seek your servant" (Psalm 119:76). He's asking God to find him. That's what a good shepherd does. He seeks the straying sheep to find and rescue. The Parable of the Lost Sheep (Luke 15:3-7) paints the portrait of the loving shepherd that leaves the 99 in search of the one that is lost. "And when he finds it, he joyfully puts it on his shoulders and goes home." There is rejoicing with friends and neighbors as the shepherd says, "'Rejoice with me; I have found my lost sheep'" (Luke 15:5-6). This parable describes the repentance of sin needed for eternal life with Jesus our Savior. It also shows the loving Master Shepherd who cares for you now.

The lost sheep discovers it is lost. It is stuck. It needs a rescuer. It doesn't know its way back. Like the sheep, you may feel lost on your grief journey. The way is not clear. Yet God seeks His sheep. He rescues them. This is where faith is seen. The Psalmist says, "For I have not forgotten your commands" (Psalm 119:176). He knows his comfort lies not in what he does or doesn't do right, but that he is marked as God's own: "Forgiven." God's Word does not change. The Truth does not change. Our position is secure. We are His! The Psalmist knows the Good Shepherd will not tire of searching for him and at just the right time will tenderly rescue him.

God's grace draws you back. He never seeks in vain. You are forever marked as His sheep if you know the Shepherd. When you feel lost, doubting, or empty know that you have a Good Shepherd who is for you as the waiting Father in the Parable of the Prodigal Son (Luke 15:11-32). He will cover you with His grace.

While I thought my husband was lost on our trip, God's eye was on him the entire time. He led me to rely on Him and trust Him for the hours ahead. He was with me in my car. About one hour later I saw my husband approaching with the U-Haul. He caught up. He found the right way. There was great rejoicing when we met at the next rest stop.

Life went on and we have kids and grandkids. God taught me that when the way feels lost His eye is forever on me. I am marked as His. And when we all get to heaven, there will be a rejoicing unlike anything you or I have ever known. Cling to it. Each day you are one day closer. It's the Truth. AMEN!

Pray: How did I get here? Lord, I'm lost! You feel far away. I feel far away. I don't even know who I am right now. Forgive me where I have doubted that You care because I know that I'm marked as Your child. When I can't find my way Your Word says You seek me out. In Your grace rescue and keep me. I need You, Lord, be glorified in me.

CrossRoads for Thought:

- *Reflect on previous times you experienced being lost or losing something/someone. What did God show you through those instances?*
- *What words would you use to describe your faith walk with God right now? Take some time and be honest with Him about how you feel. Use descriptive words. If you recognize that God is showing you things or attitudes you need to change, have a time of confession. Thank Him with words of praise for the things that describe His grace as you walk through this hard time.*
- *Meditate on Psalm 23. What are your surroundings? What is the weather? What does it feel like to picture Jesus as your Good Shepherd? What is He saying to you? How is He touching you? What is your posture? How has He marked you as His sheep? Praise Him for His grace.*

More Scriptures: Ps 23; Ps 73; Ezek 34:15-16; Lk 15:3-6; Lk 15:11-32; Lk 19:10; Jn 6:39

18. PAIN
–sorrow; pain, both mental and physical

Hebrews 12:11 *No discipline seems pleasant at the time, but painful. Later on, however, it produces a harvest of righteousness and peace for those who have been trained by it (NIV).*

"What is the pain level?" Have you been asked that before? It's an effective tool used by health professionals, parents and family members to measure the severity of pain on a scale of 1 to 10 with 10 being the highest.

I have had three occasions of intense physical pain, which thankfully ended with my three dear and healthy children. Other painful situations don't end so well. Many people have shared with me the intense pain their loved ones experienced with various types of diseases, especially cancer. You may be able to relate to that.

I have walked through another kind of pain. It was the emotional pain of grief. That pain was so intense that it caused physical pain. An example of this was in the Garden of Gethsemane when Jesus was praying to His Father before the crucifixion. His emotional pain was so great that Luke the doctor tells us in Luke 22:44, "And being in anguish, he prayed more earnestly, and his sweat was like drops of blood falling to the ground." Some scholars think this could have been a medical condition called hematidrosis, which is the actual mingling of blood and sweat as in cases of extreme anguish, strain or sensitivity (Hoerber 1593).

When we walk through the grief of losing a loved one, the pain is felt at different emotional and physical levels. There is a gut-wrenching soul pain that feels like no pain medicine can cure. Some people experience physical pain and see their doctors, as they should. Others will seek appropriate professional help, such as counselors, ministers, or psychologists. Joining a support group is a great option too. Sometimes taking a step like this can be hard, but it may be the best thing you can do when the physical or emotional pain feels like a "10" or higher. Know that these are healthy options. Remember, coping through this season of pain may be the hardest thing you will ever do. Self-care with appropriate professional steps can be the healthiest next step for you.

I'm comforted by what God says in His Word about pain and struggles. One example is Hebrews 12:11, "No discipline seems pleasant at the time, but painful." The Bible teaches that God is our loving Father. He always acts out of His heart of love for His children. This is true throughout both Old and New Testament teachings. As a loving parent He is always with us, and at times His love is displayed through discipline or correction. God doesn't correct us to punish us. Jesus suffered that for us once and for all on the cross. He does correct us with love and patience but not His justice.

The Bible does teach that there are consequences for our sins. Sin muddies the water and hinders obedience to God. God knows this and draws us back to Him by chastening us. He commands us to repent and turn away from sin. We are the light to a dying world that needs the Savior. We need to live lives of obedience and holiness for the glory of God. When we do, we give a clear witness for others to see the love of Jesus.

So how does discipline apply to grief? The word corresponding to "discipline" in the KJV is "chastening." The Greek word for "chastening" ("*paideia*") means *"whatever in adults also cultivates the soul, especially by correcting mistakes and curbing passions; instruction which aims at increasing virtue"* (Blue Letter Bible, *"paideia"*). A synonym for this word is nurture. I am NOT saying that we lost loved ones due to our sins and the grief is God's discipline to hurt us. I am saying that we are sinful people who continually need His loving instruction and nurture in ALL circumstances. His love is everlasting and never fails.

When we see that the word "discipline" applies to both times of sinful acts and times of general instruction, we can be encouraged. We have a nurturing God who takes our times of "pain" (Hebrew *"kĕ'eb"*- *"pain, both mental and physical, sorrow"*) (Blue Letter Bible, *"kĕ'eb"*) and sorrow, and uses them for our training.

The process of going *through* the pain and *through* the grief results in righteousness and peace when you are trained by it. The Greek word for "trained" ("*gymnazō*") is from the world of athletics and it is *"exercising vigorously, either the mind or the body"* (Blue Letter Bible, *"gymnazō"*). It takes a lot of vigorous mental and spiritual exercise to work through the pain of grief. Satan seeks to confuse and pull you away with his lies. The needed spiritual solution is to "work-out" in the Scriptures. Rom 12:2b says, "Be transformed by the renewing of your mind." That comes with some "Word work-outs."

You have to trust that whatever grief God has permitted to come your way is being used by Him to train you. Too often people want to rush through the pain. Understandable! Who likes to hurt? The question is asked, "When will this grief and pain be done?" It is not the "being done with grief" that is the right question. For a Christian the right question is, "How will God change me and make me more holy through this?" The answer is to be honest with God about the pain and be drawn into His holiness and intimacy through it, which is being trained by it for righteousness and peace. Look at Hebrews 12:11-14. It speaks of God's holiness and how you are His examples to others. This comes as we are trained, changed, and used for His glory. His discipline will equip you to help others.

You can see God's holiness coming through others impacted by grief. God's righteousness and peace in you will help others who grieve. As you are trained by God and comforted in your own grief and pain, you can reflect a renewed awareness of Him and minister comfort to others. You can live out the truth of 2 Corinthians 1:3-5, "we can comfort those in any trouble with the comfort we ourselves have received from God."

So what is your grief pain level today? Tell God the number of your grief pain. Trust that He has just the right dose of what you need. No wonder shot or wonder drug compares to His love and care for you.

Pray: My pain is so severe at times. I feel like You don't hear me since it seems to get worse. I do believe You love me and will not give me more pain than I can bear. I do believe You are with me and haven't forsaken me. Help me to know You more through this. I am weak and need Your spiritual training in the Word. Lead me, Lord, and teach me to trust in You.

CrossRoads for Thought:

- *Go to a safe person you can be honest with and share your grief pain level number. Pray together.*
- *Are you having a daily "Word work-out?" If you don't know how, learn to use a concordance or online Bible tool and begin looking up the 30 words in this book. Don't rush the process. You may need to spend one week on each word. Ask the Lord for truths to renew your mind. Journal it.*
- *Think of someone you know who has been "trained" through grief to comfort others with God's comfort. Go out for coffee or lunch together and ask to hear that person's story. Ask "How is your experience making you more holy?"*

More Scriptures: Rom 5:3-5; 2 Tim 3:16-17; Heb 12; Jam 1:2-4

19. PRAY
–entreat, make intercession for anyone (Also PRAYER)

<u>Romans 8:26</u> *In the same way, the Spirit helps us in our weakness. We do not know what we ought to pray for, but the Spirit himself intercedes for us with groans that words cannot express (NIV).*

*H*ave you ever had someone older and wiser step in and defend you? Yes, of course you have. It may have been a parent, a sibling, a friend, a lawyer, or a teacher. How did that feel? Didn't it feel good? Like someone had your back, right? Have you also been the person to defend someone else? Others feel safety and assurance when you can come alongside and support them.

When you began a grief journey you may not have had someone to walk alongside you to shield and defend you from unwanted conversations or situations. It hurts when someone tries to help but says the wrong thing. It makes you hurt more. Oh! Having a shield at times like that would be helpful. The negative words or situations would bounce off the shield and never touch your soul.

You may not have a shield, but you do have a beautiful defense that God has given. You have the ever available gift of prayer. At any moment in time you have the privilege of prayer as your best shield and defense.

Paul tells us that when we don't know what we should pray for, the Spirit Himself intercedes for us in ways that words can't express. I've been there. There were no words to express the depth of the pain, concern, or heartache. It is precisely at times like that when we can depend upon the Lord beyond our understanding. We don't have to understand. We just need to trust that He will do what is best for us at all times. In verse 27 Paul says that "the Spirit intercedes for God's people in accordance with God's will."

It gets better. God exists in three Persons, the Father, the Son, and the Holy Spirit. It is by the Holy Spirit that we come to know God. He reveals truth to us from His Word. God the Father's great love for us is revealed in the person of Jesus the Son. The Son loved us so much that He left heaven to become one of us. God's Son was our ultimate Defender and Shield.

It gets even better. Because Jesus left heaven and came to earth in a human body, He had a dual nature. He was both God and man. But He had no sin. He lived a perfect life. No one else has ever done that. Only Jesus! No one else said He would die and three days later come back to life. Jesus did! Because He lives we will live with Him forever.

What about the times when life is really hard and the grief is too intense for you to pray? The Spirit intercedes for you. Romans 8:34 says, "Christ Jesus who died – more than that, who was raised to life – is at the right hand of God and is also interceding for us." Hebrews 7:25 says, "Therefore he is able to save completely those who come to God through him, because he always lives to intercede for them."

Jesus, who is both God and man, lives to intercede for you. The Greek word here for "intercede" (*"entygchanō"*) means *"to pray, entreat, make intercession for any one"* (Blue Letter Bible, *"entygchanō"*). When we "pray" (*"proseuchomai"*) meaning *"to offer prayers"* (Blue Letter Bible, *"proseuchomai"*), we come to God through Him. In the verses prior to and also in verse 25, it talks about Jesus being a perfect High Priest. In the Old Testament, the High Priest was the only person that could offer sacrifices for the sins of the people. He was the mediator, the go-between before a perfect God and the sinful people. Yet the High Priest himself had sin and had to offer up sacrifices for his own sin. But not Jesus. He is the perfect High Priest, both God and human.

Because He was human, He is our best Defender who really does understand, including the pain and struggles of grief. Hebrews 4:14-16 states clearly why we can have confidence in our prayers being heard. Read it, especially vv. 15 and 16. "For we do not have a high priest who is unable to sympathize with our weaknesses, but we have one who has been tempted in every way, just as we are – yet was without sin. Let us then approach the throne of grace with confidence, so that we may receive mercy and find grace to help us in our time of need."

Jesus "gets" you. He lived a human life. He is able to sympathize with your weaknesses and temptations. He knows what it is like to experience a grief far worse than you or I will ever know. He experienced the grief of having His Father turn His back on Him because of our sin. The price of sin for all had to be paid by a perfect sacrifice. Jesus willingly did that. He is our Defender, our perfect High Priest.

We can approach the throne of grace with confidence to receive mercy and grace to help us in our time of need (Hebrews 4:16). You can be assured and confident of God's help. Jesus knows how hard grief can be. He is the perfect High Priest to represent my case to the Father so that I can find help in my time of need. Go to the Father, through the Son, by the Holy Spirit.

Your prayers don't have to be perfect. God searches hearts and knows the depths of pain. Isn't it a great help to know that Jesus is interceding for you? No one loves you more than Jesus. Prayer is God's gift to you. Jesus intercedes and "gets" you, especially in your time of need.

Pray: Jesus, what a comfort to know that I can come to You in my time of need and You sympathize with me. You understand. Lord, You loved me so much that You died for me. Now my heart is broken and I don't even know what to say because it hurts so much. Help me! Send Your Holy Spirit to pray for me when I have no energy or words. I come. I'm here. I believe You will give me mercy and grace because I am in desperate need. Hear my prayer. Help!

CrossRoads for Thought:

- *Have you had times when you know God heard your prayers? What happened? Recall them and write them down for future encouragement.*
- *What a gift prayer is. Tell God what it means to you to be able to pray to Him. Think of all the many things that are good that you daily experience. Use the alphabet and go through A to Z. List things you are thankful for, e.g., apples, brakes, children, etc. Pray thanks to God for each one. Watch for your perspective to change.*
- *Can you picture Jesus as your Defender, waiting to hear you and represent you? Can you picture what He is doing? His expression? If you could talk face to face to Jesus, what would you say? What would He say back to you? Write it down. Turn it into a prayer to Him.*

More Scriptures: Matt 6:5-15; Rom 8:26-27; Rom 8:34; Phil 4:6-7; Heb 4:14-16; Heb 7:25

20. TRUST
–to have confidence, to be secure

Psalm 91:2 *I will say of the Lord, "He is my refuge and my fortress, my God, in whom I trust" (NIV).*

I have loved roller-coasters since I was a kid. I enjoy seeing the adrenaline high in people exiting the seats with their faces excitedly thrilled from their heart-pumping experiences. I admit, however, that if I ever see horrified faces on those departing, I might have mixed feelings about the next coaster ride. But I will trust the roller-coaster to deliver me safe and sound to exit in several minutes. Otherwise, I will never get on one again.

Like a roller-coaster ride, you may have thought you planned life and could see where it would take you. You never thought you would embark upon a journey that looks like it does now. Grief is like that. It is the reality of living out a dream that was shattered by death or whatever you thought your hoped and preferred future was supposed to be. It may feel like you have entered a grief roller-coaster and you have no idea where it will go, when it will dip, where it will turn, or if you will ever reach the end.

Along this up and down journey, you know others who are there for you and others who aren't. Death changes things and some people don't know how to handle grief. They just stop communicating or avoid the subject. They may be clueless about how to support you. When you've asked for their support, they failed to deliver. You no longer trust them to help you. It hurts!

It hurts terribly, especially if you feel betrayed by a close friend or family member. It makes you want to just wall yourself in and never trust again. Grief has already made you feel different. It can seem to require more energy to trust than to stay alone in your pain. If you feel like one who betrayed you is God, where do you turn then? Stop! This is when the enemy Satan can cause confusion in the matter of trust.

You may *feel* like God betrayed you but the truth is you can always trust Him. Just as Satan twisted the truth with Adam and Eve, he will attempt to do that until the end of time. You, however, can trust in God regardless of your circumstances.

There are countless Scripture verses that talk about trusting in God. One Hebrew word for "trust" *("batach")* meaning *"to have confidence, to be secure"* (Blue Letter Bible, *"batach"*) does not picture something we manufacture. Faith is a gift of God. In Psalm 22:9 David says of God, "Yet you brought me out of the womb; you made me trust in you." The Psalmist often recounts to God his situation, but he then recalls his trust in the name of the Lord. At times it seems like he is talking faith and trust words to himself, as if he is standing in front of a mirror and talking to God. There is power in speaking these words of faith. When you do you are calling to mind the truth, which trumps the lies of the enemy.

One of my favorite ways to build trust in God is to pray Ephesians 6:14-17 silently, or even better, out loud. Ephesians 6:10-18 is subtitled in some Bibles as "The Armor of God." It is a great passage for in-depth study to learn each of the weapons used for spiritual warfare. As a Christian you are currently involved in a spiritual battle. Verse 12 states, "For our struggle is not against flesh and blood, but against the rulers, against the authorities, against the powers of this dark world and against the spiritual forces of evil in the heavenly realms." We can't see that world with our eyes; it is discerned by the Spirit of God. When you are hurting, Satan loves to come and cause you to be confused, isolated and mistrusting of God.

Ephesians 6:10-18 encourages you to stand strong in the Lord. It explains how to arm yourself for battle. You put on the full armor of God: the belt of truth on your waist, the breastplate of righteousness, your feet fitted with the gospel of peace, the shield of faith, the helmet of salvation and the sword of the Spirit. All but one are defensive weapons to ward off the attacks of Satan. There is one offensive weapon – the sword of the Spirit, which is the Word of God.

The Greek meaning is powerful and more descriptive in helping you see the power God gives you to do battle. In verse 17 the "sword" *("machaira")* of the Spirit is a *"short straight sword used for thrusting"* and could provide deadly attacks (Blue Letter Bible, *"machaira"*). The "word" of God *("rhēma")* is a specific word, an *"individual scripture which the Spirit brings to our remembrance for use in time of need, a prerequisite being the regular storing of the mind with Scripture"* (Vine, "word"). It is a "now" Word from God. Jesus exemplified this concept when He was tempted by Satan in the desert. He countered every attack of Satan by stating, *"It is written..."* He defeated Satan by countering him with the specific now words from Scripture verses. The truth of God defeated the enemy who twisted God's Word.

Do what Jesus did. Recognize that God has equipped you to do spiritual battle. Use the Word and pray protection over yourself and your loved ones by praying these pieces of God's armor in place. Strengthen your faith and trust in God by recognizing His power in battle with you. We offensively fight and give deadly defeat to the lies of the enemy with the "rhema" - now Word of God. Ask God to bring to mind the Scripture you need. Recite in your mind, "It is written..." If you are new to knowing God and His Word, ask Him to help you find words of faith in a concordance or an online resource. He will guide your steps. "And pray in the Spirit on all occasions" (Ephesians 6:18). This defeats the enemy with the tools God gives – prayer and the Word.

The roller-coaster of life does have someone in charge. God knows exactly where your ride is going, who you will encounter along the way, and where it will end. You can trust Him and His ways even when the pathway is scary, lonely, and long. The end will result in an arrival into a glorious place you can't even imagine. No theme park ride can compare. Nothing in life can separate us from that time. Read Romans 8:31-39. So be it, Lord. Amen!

Pray: I have been hurt in the area of trust. Having said that, I'm not even sure I can trust You, Lord. Protect my mind from the lies of Satan that would cause me to distrust Your ways when they do not make sense to me. Help me trust You, no matter what happens.

CrossRoads for Thought:

- *Daily pray on "the armor of God" from Ephesians 6:11-18. Simplify your prayer as you memorize each piece. Visualize Jesus placing His protection on you with each piece.*
- *How are you doing in the grief trust area? Have you been wounded by others? Are you isolating yourself? Are you letting others help you with your grief? Ask God to help you deal with any areas of hurt from the past. Unforgiveness binds you up and keeps you from trusting again. Ask Him to guide you to healthy places of trust.*
- *Psalm 91 is known as the 9-1-1 Psalm – great for emergencies. Note repeated words in the Psalm. Find all the times "will" is used. Make note of each one for encouragement and how you can trust God.*

More Scriptures: Ps 9:10; Ps 30:5, Ps 32:10; Ps 56:3-4; Prov 3:5; Is 26:3-4; 2 Cor 10:4-5

21. ACCEPTANCE
–reception; admission

Job 2:10 *He replied, "You are talking like a foolish woman. Shall we accept good from God, and not trouble?" In all this, Job did not sin in what he said (NIV).*

Say these two words carefully – "except" and "accept." Although sounding almost identical, these words are very different in meaning. If you are navigating the loss of someone you love you probably are catching yourself saying the first one more. Statements like: "We planned to go on this trip, *except*…" "We had just retired and were in the process of moving to a smaller home, *except*…" or "She was fine one day, *except*…" You know how the rest of the sentence goes.

While dealing with your grief, you may have well-meaning friends ask you, "When do you think you will 'get over' it – you know, the loss of your loved one? How long has it been now?" Maybe they haven't said it bluntly, but no doubt the implication is there. With the passing of time people assume you will be "getting over it." But wait! It's not a "getting over" the loss. You don't "get over" love. This is wounding terminology. It's not like a cold or the flu – one day there and the next day you are "over it." No way!

So when does the word "accept" come into the picture? Where the word "except" can be more negative, the word "accept" and "acceptance" have the opposite effect.

Acceptance is a needed part of a grief journey. It is that time when the loss of your loved one is assimilated and you know you will be OK. And it is OK that you will be OK. In fact, it is good. You still grieve and love, but you are making it and that feels good. With hard work and time there is "hope" for your future and grief recovery.

Time for a caution. If you are at the beginning of a grief journey, to say that one day you will be OK can feel impossible. You may even question that you will make it. That's normal. As impossible as it may feel to see, it is a process to get there and you are on the way. Hard work and time will get you there with hope providing the fuel. While you cannot see your loved one, you will find a new way to hold that love that will be healing and safe. It's all a part of finding acceptance and living life with a new level of depth and meaning.

In some grief literature, you may run into others terms for acceptance. You may hear assimilation of the loss, integration of the loss, grief healing, grief recovery, or grief reconciliation. The concept is the same – a receiving of the death and loss and allowing your life to be changed by it in a healthy way. Since grief work is individualistic, this is not something to wrap into a time frame with set rules, stages, and expectations. Recognize that missing your loved one is never done; you will always have those times when grief hits, no matter how much time has passed. The process of learning from your grief may continue your entire life.

The most challenging book in the Bible that deals with grief is the book of Job. It paints a picture of an incredible man of faith who had to endure extreme grief. He had a loving marriage, ten children, limitless wealth, and a love of God unequaled in his day. The Lord said of Job, "There is no one on earth like him; he is blameless and upright, a man who fears God and shuns evil" (Job 1:8).

We see the heavenly battle between God and Satan, who questions Job's love of God. Why wouldn't Job love God since he had so many blessings? God allowed Job to be tested by Satan within limits. God intended Job's greater good and His own glory. And so we read and learn.

First, Satan strikes Job with the death of all of his children and the loss of all of his wealth. Instead of bashing God in his grief, Job knelt and worshiped Him. He says in Job 1:21, *"The Lord gave and the Lord has taken away; may the name of the Lord be praised."* Wow! What stupendous faith!

Second, Satan continues his attack on Job with extreme pain and sickness, but Job never gives up on his conviction that God is good in spite of suffering and adversity. When his wife encouraged him to curse God and die, he spoke a tremendous statement of faith. In Job 2:10 he says, "Shall we accept good from God, and not trouble?" The Word goes on to say, "In all this, Job did not sin in what he said."

"Shall we accept good from God, and not trouble" (Job 2:10)? The Hebrew for "accept" (*"qabal"*) meaning *"to take, receive, be before"* (Blue Letter Bible, *"qabal"*) is a receiving – receiving of both good and trouble. For grief acceptance to take place requires open hands to receive – to receive from God both the good and the bad. It is a humbling recognition that He is God and we are not. Think about it. We deserve no good thing. But God loved us so much, and sent His own Son as a sacrifice to pay our sin debt.

We receive good things along with pain. Life is not easy, but blessings we don't deserve abound. God delights in blessing His children while also working His glory through painful times. We can glorify Him and we can witness to others through blessings that come with trials. He works through us in spite of our sin and weaknesses. It is amazing grace.

Think about what Job knew. He was simply relying on his strong conviction of God's love and goodness, offering praise and statements of faith in the midst of his grief and pain. The truth is that God exists over us in the heavenly realm. While aware of things unseen and unknown by us, He is always working for our good and His glory. Some of His greatest works are during pain and suffering.

Job's life sets an example of a godly man of faith. Many Christians may think it is too unrealistic to feel as he felt. In the entire book of Job we see his honest dialogue and struggles with God and his friends. He sets a high example. But there is one particular principle of his faith that is simple; it may seem too difficult to be real. To move through your grief in a healthy way requires an openness of your hands to receive from God by faith all that lies ahead. In your grief and pain you can join with Job and say, "Blessed be the name of the Lord" (Job 1:21, NASB). Say to God, "You are God and I am not. I choose to trust this pathway to You and receive the training that You will give me. Help me have faith to believe and a heart open to receive in the midst of my pain."

In the Chinese language the word for "crisis" has a double meaning – both danger and opportunity. You can trust that God is working through this crisis of death as an "opportunity" to refine you, so that you may glorify Him more clearly and love Him more dearly. There are no "exceptions" as we all will pass through good and bad. Will you "accept" that God's loving hand will sustain you throughout this journey?

Job trusted God's goodness and God rewarded him beyond his previous blessings. Your greatest reward will be in heaven. Meanwhile, "accept" that God's plan is at work in you in ways you never thought you would know. Job did. He is an example of God's faithfulness.

Pray: Lord, I'm here to receive from You. My hands are trembling but I'm choosing to open them to you as symbolic of my heart opening to You. Take me on this journey through my grief. I don't know where I'm going but I know that You can take me to a place of healing and change along the way. I trust that "acceptance" will come in its time; cause it to be on a pathway and timeline You will direct. I'm too tired to figure it out. As Job did by faith I say, "Blessed be Your name, in me, Lord, in me, please!"

CrossRoads for Thought:

- *Be still and quiet before the Lord in a position of humility and openness. You can kneel or sit. Pray with hands open before God to receive. Confess honestly any emotions toward God that are affecting you in an unhealthy way. Say, "Lord, I confess...." After confession, say, "Lord, I receive your forgiveness for...." After forgiveness, say, "Holy Spirit, I'm here to receive. Fill me." With hands open to God, quietly wait to receive what God may give you.*

- *Take some time this week and read through the book of Job. If you can, read sources for any hard to understand sections. What questions do you have of God? Use some quiet time to ask Him. Listen to Him for truths He will show you. What can you apply from this section of Scripture to your grief?*

- *What Christian do you know who has gone through grief in a healthy way? Ask for a time to meet. Make a list and with permission ask any questions that will benefit you in your journey. Don't be afraid to ask what went well and what didn't go well. Ask for examples. What does acceptance, integration, or assimilation mean to that person?*

More Scriptures: Ps 23:3-4; Pr 2:1-7; Pr 19:20; Is 61:1-3; Rom 8:28; 2 Thes 1:11-12

22. GRIEF
–sorrow, pain, of persons mourning

<u>John 16:22</u> *"So with you: Now is your time of grief, but I will see you again and you will rejoice, and no one will take away your joy" (NIV).*

I have a hard time waiting for surprises. My daughter is worse than I am. If she knows there's something "cooking," she'll begin her investigative process to figure it out. She's a "Curious George." It is hard to surprise her. We have pulled it off very few times. What a joy to see her when she is "surprised."

What do you think it is about surprises that makes them so hard? I think it is the waiting. Waiting = patience. Yikes! Not good at this, and I'm not alone. As time passes our society becomes overall more impatient. Do you find yourself getting irritated when the computer doesn't respond as quickly as you think it should? What if you are stuck in traffic by an accident ahead and not able to get where you need to be on time? It is beyond your control. Our technologically bound society can be quickly stifled when technology breaks down. My lack of patience at such times quickly manifests its ugly presence.

Jesus knew His disciples would be surprised and challenged by His upcoming crucifixion. He knew they would become confused and grieve. But He also knew their future joy after His resurrection. He encouraged them by giving some powerful words of preparation before He died.

In John 16:20-22 Jesus said they would weep and mourn, while the world rejoiced; but their "grief" ("*lypē*") meaning *"sorrow, pain, grief, annoyance, affliction, of persons mourning"* (Blue Letter Bible, "*lypē*") would turn to joy. He then compared it to a woman giving birth to a baby; she has pain because it is time to deliver her child. After the birth the mother forgets the pain and rejoices.

If you have suffered the loss of a child through miscarriage, stillbirth, or an early death, the sting of these words is even more piercing. The joy you anticipated never came to counter the pain. Instead, it was multiplied by grief. For some who have experienced healthy children, your joy later turned to sorrow as that child died far earlier than you ever dreamed. Your pain of grief was so great that you wondered why it happened to you. Many can relate to that deep grief.

If you have been blessed with the birth of one or more children, you can identify with these words. You quickly forgot the pain of birth with the arrival of the new child to love. Jesus used this example to remind His disciples that He would soon leave and it would be their time for grief. Their pain of loss would be unimaginable. But they would rejoice again. He would rise from death and the impact would be beyond all they could imagine.

It is important to note what Jesus told the disciples. He promised to send the Holy Spirit (John 14:16, 26). He said more in John 16:7, "It is for your good that I am going away. Unless I go away, the Counselor will not come to you; but if I go, I will send him to you." He goes on in John 16:13-14, "But when he, the Spirit of truth, comes, he will guide you into all truth. He will not speak on his own; he will speak only what he hears, and he will tell you what is yet to come. He will bring glory to me by taking from what is mine and making it known to you."

The Holy Spirit, whom Jesus sent "will guide you into all truth...He will tell you what is yet to come" (John 16:13). By revealing Jesus' truth to you the Holy Spirit will bring Jesus glory. If you are a believer in Jesus Christ, His Holy Spirit resides in you. He will bring truth into your life situation where you hurt, doubt, grieve, and question. He is the revealer of Jesus. He faithfully reveals Himself through prayer and Scripture.

You are in this in-between time similar to the disciples. You are doing life and "stuff" in life happens. Disappointments occur, jobs are lost, the economic situation grows bleak, and death happens. You hurt; you grieve. But just as Jesus promised, your current grief will turn to joy. You have the promised Holy Spirit to reveal Jesus. God loves you and will reveal Himself to you. How? You ask. You pray. You turn to the Word. You expect.

If you grow impatient with the grieving process, stop and ask, "What, Lord, are You showing me? Let me see in this moment what You would have me see. Help me wait on your Holy Spirit to speak to my spirit." Pray Psalm 119:18, "Open my eyes that I may see wonderful things in your law." Turn to the Scriptures. Listen not with your ears but with your spirit. If you are new to this, just read, pause, meditate, and quiet your mind and spirit. Ask God what He wants to say to you. Take time. Learning to hear God's voice can't be rushed.

Come as a little child with a heart expecting and waiting to be surprised with the joy by the Spirit's presence. There may be a quiet inner voice or it might be a word or verse that jumps off the page of the Bible. But you will know that it is not a coincidence. It is a "God-incident." He is speaking His truth to you. Keep doing this regularly, getting to know God's Word and how He speaks to you through it and prayer. Watch and listen.

Read John 14:2-3. You can't imagine the "surprise of heaven yet to be revealed." This time of grief is quickly passing when viewed from that perspective. You can't see it all yet. God has given you only a small measure of the joy that awaits. While this present grief is so hard at times, the best is yet to come. We will rejoice together. Be ever patient. God will see us and He will see your joy that day. He's waiting for more of His children. In His time...in His perfect time.

<u>Pray:</u> *While I know heaven awaits, living on earth is a day by day process of walking through the grief and pain. You know how hard it can be on earth, Jesus. Thank You for not only dying for me, but also for becoming like me, understanding the depth of my hurt. Knowing You have given me the Holy Spirit to guide my prayers is such a comfort. You know my grief. Here I am. Help again!*

CrossRoads for Thought:

- *How could God surprise you? Talk to him about your needs. Pray. Read the Word.*
- *Pick another person who is grieving. Ask God to give you a unique idea of how to anonymously surprise them. Do it and then think about what you can do next week to surprise someone else. No telling anyone. Just you and God should know.*
- *One way that the Holy Spirit glorifies Jesus is through your testimony? Do you know someone who doesn't know Jesus as Savior? Pray and ask God if there is someone you can pray for. What does He want you to share about Him, your faith, or truths you are learning, especially as you go through this journey of grief?*

More Scriptures: Ps 10:14; Ps 31:9; Ps 88:9; Lam 3:32-33; 2 Tim 3:15-16; 1 Pet 1:6-7

23. GUILT
–iniquity, feeling of responsibility or remorse for some offense
(Also GUILTY)

Psalm 32:5 *Then I acknowledged my sin to you and did not cover up my iniquity. I said, "I will confess my transgressions to the LORD" – and you forgave the guilt of my sin (NIV).*

*O*uch! You rub your hands together and you feel it. You look but you see nothing. Yet as you rub your finger over the spot, you feel it again. Ouch! That sharp little splinter. Since you can't see it you try to ignore it. But it isn't going away. The next day the finger is hurting more and the area around the splinter is pink and inflamed. So you get the tweezers. But it's in there deep and it's hard to see. You try as hard as you can but you can't get the edge of it. How can such a little thing be such a pain and nuisance? Now you have an infected finger.

The guilt and unforgiveness experienced with grief can be like that splinter. It may not be a big thing, but it can fester and cause so much hurt and pain. If only you could get it out and never remember it. If it were only that easy. Instead, the poison of the area infected with guilt can take over your emotions. Soon your grief swells with self-loathing and wishing you could redo the past. You beat yourself up for what you did or did not do.

Why are you bound up with guilt? Are you so guilt-ridden about how you treated your hard-to-deal-with ill loved one and now you can't stop? Perhaps it was an angry statement you made and now you can't say you are sorry. You may be upset with your friends who do not call or visit anymore. Finally when one of them called, you burst out in angry, blaming statements. Grief and guilt are so messy.

God understands guilt and can even have a good purpose for it. David wrote about guilt and forgiveness in the Psalms. David was human; he struggled with sin and guilt. Because of his sin of adultery with Bathsheba, David experienced the death of a child. He understood grief in many ways through losing friendships, sons, etc. God drew near to David. David loved Him. This "man after God's heart" (Acts 13:22) understood how to deal with guilt and receive forgiveness. Read Psalm 32:1-5. David wrote about the weight of his own sin and guilt. "When I kept silent, my bones wasted away through my groaning all day long. For day and night your hand was heavy upon me; my strength was sapped as in the heat of summer" (vv. 3-4).

When sin is not dealt with and ignored or covered up, you can become physically and emotionally sick. It becomes a heavy load which will sap your strength. We all have felt it. We all have sinned and fallen short of the glory of God (Romans 3:23). That is why Jesus came. By His death He paid the price for our sin and guilt; He puts sinners into a right relationship with God.

God designed us to hate sin and its consequences. When we transgress God's perfect laws, we separate ourselves from Him. Out of love for us He sends conviction by the Holy Spirit to bring us back to Him. The Holy Spirit makes us uncomfortable so that we can desire to turn from sin and repent. We must let conviction bring about the good work of repentance. If we do we learn His response to us, which is FORGIVENESS.

David says, "Then I acknowledged my sin to you and did not cover up my iniquity. I said 'I will confess my transgressions to the Lord' – and you forgave the guilt of my sin" (v. 5). This is God's answer for dealing with guilt. He doesn't just forgive us of the sin; He also heals the guilt of the sin. Here the Hebrew for "guilt "or "iniquity" is "`avon" meaning *"perversity, depravity, iniquity, guilt or punishment of iniquity; consequence of or punishment for iniquity"* (Blue Letter Bible, "`avon"). It is the sin, the depravity, guilt, and consequences of the sin that can make us sick. Who of us has not felt this bitter aftertaste of sin? That's what guilt is – it's that on-going feeling that festers and gets bigger and sicker, like that infected finger with the splinter.

In dealing with grief, you can run into regrets and guilt. There is a very close relationship between regrets and guilt. Regret is discussed under that word, but I will differentiate here.

- Regrets are the things you wish you had said or done.
- Guilt is what you feel when you believe you have done something wrong (Fitzgerald 92).

"Guilt is a feeling of responsibility or remorse felt for some offense, crime, wrong, etc., whether real or imagined" ("Def. "guilt"). Guilt can take over when you live in the "I wish" and "if only" of regrets. Others may try to minimize your feelings of guilt by telling you that you shouldn't feel the way you do. While they mean well, it doesn't help with the guilt. Guilt needs honest acknowledgement of your feelings to be processed.

Understand if the guilt is coming from God or Satan. Here's how you can know:

1. Guilt from the Holy Spirit is a good and loving emotion. That guilt is conviction of sin, which leads to repentance. God does not want you trapped in your sin. While processing guilt is never fun or easy, it leads to healing. Confession, repentance, and turning away from it brings freedom.

2. In contrast, guilt from Satan is bad; it is meant to shame you and condemn you, while beating you up and reminding you of how bad you are. It traps and ensnares you. It is a lie used to prevent Christians from being effective witnesses for our Lord. He traps you into thinking it is all about you, which causes you to search for answers that never satisfy. It is a feeling of never being happy because you did something wrong. You deserve this pain. All LIES!

Satan brings condemnation with guilt; God brings forgiveness and freedom through confession of guilt. David wrote in Psalm 32:1, "Blessed is he whose transgressions are forgiven, whose sins are covered." You, although bereaved, can be blessed and forgiven. You who do not have to dwell in guilt about what you did or didn't do.

There is another noteworthy warning connected with guilt. You must realize that after confession and repentance of your guilt you are free. Guilt likes to come back and take up the place formerly occupied. Satan has no rightful place where God has forgiven. Shut the door. Reject the lies. Guilt has a way of covering every thought with its effects again. This is simple in principle but can be hard to practice. Don't open the door; don't go there in your thoughts. Read and remember 1 John 4:4b, "the one who is in you is greater than the one who is in the world." That will help.

Make this area open to the tweezers of the Holy Spirit. He has the best medicine for any infection of guilt related to your grief. Go to Him.

Pray: Lord, my thoughts often go to people, places or instances I feel bad about. I keep replaying them in my mind. I know I am making myself sick with guilt. Help me identify those areas where I need to forgive myself, or where I need to forgive others. My loved one would not want me to be in this much pain and would have forgiven me. Holy Spirit, I only want to hear You. Help me, Lord.

CrossRoads for Thought:

- *Since dealing with guilt requires confession, take this as an opportunity to use a big eraser over your life. Write down the name of anyone you feel you have not forgiven. Is that person you? This is a day of forgiveness. Ask God what you can do to take one step toward forgiveness. Then do it. It may be praying, calling, writing a letter, confessing to a friend, etc. Take that step. Ask God for the next.*
- *Find a red marker. With black ink write down matters of guilt that have troubled you. It may be things like: reminding you that you were not patient; reminding you of instances where you said bad things or thought bad thoughts. Continue writing until you have exhausted all areas. If you have not prayed confession over any sin connected with these, do that now. When done take the red marker and write 1 John 1:9 over each notation. Jesus' blood covered the guilt of any of those sins. Write "FORGIVEN" in capital letters and today's date.*
- *Clean. Clean out your house, your car, your office. Pray the entire time with thanks that God's love through Jesus covered any guilt you had.*

<u>More Scriptures:</u> 2 Sam 24:10; Ezra 9:6-15; Ps 38:4; Heb 2:14-18; Heb 10:22; 1 Jn 2:1-2

24. HEAL
–to cure, to make whole
(Also HEALING)

<u>Luke 4:18-19</u> *"The Spirit of the Lord is upon me, because he hath anointed me to preach the gospel to the poor; he hath sent me to heal the brokenhearted, to preach deliverance to the captives, and recovering of sight to the blind, to set at liberty them that are bruised, to preach the acceptable year of the Lord" (KJV).*

*I*t is amazing how God has made our bodies. They repair themselves in many ways. When you get a cut, you bleed; the blood clots and then it forms a scab. The scab stays in place for several days, helping the wounded area to heal. The scab comes off and new skin has formed. If the wound was a deep cut, there may be a visible scar remaining as a reminder of the injury. Otherwise, there will be no visible way to know years later that a cut was once there.

An analogy can be made between grief and a healing wound. When it happens the cut hurts and oozes with much pain. It is a process that takes time for it to heal. Renewed pain can occur while it is healing if the scab comes off too soon. If not properly cared for, it will not heal correctly. When the cut is deeper it will retain a scar as a reminder of when the wound occurred. All these things can be true of grief as well. Read back through them as a reminder.

149

Some facts about wounds don't apply to grief. Scars usually appear within a predictable period of time. A cut results in physical pain. It can be treated clinically with medicine. In contrast the healing for grief can be unpredictable from one person to another. Grief is primarily an emotional pain, but the healing process can be greatly impacted by both physical and emotional feelings. It is an individualized journey that must be navigated.

I'm so glad that Jesus came to heal us. A summary of our Scripture (Luke 4:18-19) is that He came to heal the brokenhearted and to preach the gospel of deliverance. This verse says that He heals the brokenhearted. The Greek for "heal" ("*iaomai*") means *"to cure, to heal, to make whole"* (Blue Letter Bible, *"iaomai"*). Brokenhearted is made up of two Greek words, "broken" *("syntribō")* and "hearted" *("kardia")*. The two together mean "to tear *one's body and shatter one's strength; to suffer extreme sorrow and be, as it were, crushed" ("syntribō")* (Blue Letter Bible, *"syntribō")* and *"of the soul so far as it is affected and stirred in a bad way or good, or of the soul as the seat of the sensibilities, affections, emotions, desires, appetites, passions" ("kardia")* (Blue Letter Bible, *"kardia"*). This describes grief. Grief is that tearing of the body and shattering the strength of a person down to the very soul. Jesus came to heal that brokenheartedness.

Often I'm asked, "How long will it take to heal?" There is no one set of words to describe the process of navigating the grief. Some use the words "healing of the grief," "grief reconciliation," or "grief recovery." There is a healthy place you can get to on your grief journey where the pain is not as severe. You are a changed person, and you can weather through the major storms of the grief. You will continue to think about and miss your loved one, but that is OK. Some people think they will never get to that point but they do. It may feel impossible. Cling to HOPE. I see it happen all the time.

What is necessary to heal through grief? There are a lot of things that bring healing but let me suggest four "outs" that tend to keep people on the healing path. There are lots more things that could be said but these four are easier to remember. You will have to feel through your pain to heal. I say, "You must feel to heal." You can't numb your pain or go around it. It must be embraced by you to become healthy. Yet you can't feel your pain 24/7. There will be times when you will have it in the front of your mind and you will be feeling it; at other times you will have it in the back of your mind so you do not feel the pain continually. Every day will be different and you will find what works best for you. Some days will be harder grief days; other days will be better. Grief is very much like a roller-coaster. This is so normal.

Here are four healthy "outs" for you to use:

1. Talk it out – Identify some "safe" people with whom you can be real. They should be good listeners who care about you and are NOT trying to "fix" you. Most often (there

can be exceptions) they should not be family members as they are experiencing the loss too but from a different perspective (e.g., child, parent, etc.). You may only need one or two safe people that you can rely on and be real with. The best ones are those who have been through a similar type of loss.

2. <u>Cry it out</u> – Tears are a great stress reliever. God gave our bodies tear ducts for a reason. Tears can cleanse us with emotions that are important. If they don't come OUT, they stay IN; IN can equal stress and can make you sick. By crying you mourn and release emotions related to the one you lost. It's OK to cry. It can make you feel better. Some people cry a lot; some people cry little but feel it inside. The point is: If you need to cry, it is healthy and OK to cry. Do it. If you feel better crying in private, that is understandable.

3. <u>Write it out</u> – Journaling is an effective tool to express the emotions you are feeling. It feels good for some reason to take feelings that are swimming around in the head and get them on paper. You may not journal but perhaps prefer art or music to expression your grief feelings. Here are three ways for journaling:

   a. *Two sentences a day* – Write two sentences each day about how you are doing on your grief journey. If possible write these sentences the same time each day. Reflect back on what happened in the last 24 hours. The first sentence is <u>negative.</u> It is a "venting" statement and in it you express what has hurt you, made you sad, mad, and angry, etc., within the last day. You should be "real" here. The second sentence is <u>positive.</u> It expresses something good that happened in the last 24 hours. It was what blessed you or made you see something good. You should dwell on the positive sentence. Both sentences have to reflect on something which affected your grief, negative and then positive.

b. *Writing to God* – Choose a section of Scripture and read it. The Psalms are wonderful for this. Slow down and meditate on it. Tell God how you are really feeling by writing to Him. If you feel hurt, angry, comforted, blessed, hopeless, etc., write it. Reflect on how the Scripture helped you. Tell God all that you feel. Be quiet and listen for His Holy Spirit to speak to you. Wait upon God as you are quiet before Him.

c. *Write to your loved one* – Many people talk to their loved ones in some form or another: at the gravesite, within the home, etc. Writing is another form of talking to your loved one that can feel comforting. You pour out your feelings in a way that is different. (*This must not be an expectation for the deceased to talk back*). Writing can be especially good after highly emotional days such as birthdays, anniversaries, holidays, or other times when you typically would have been with your loved one. You can journal weekly, daily, or just whenever it feels like it will help. What you write can include all emotions: sadness, anger, joy, blessings, etc. You must be honest. You can keep this journal or shred it when you desire. The process of doing the writing is when most of the healing takes place.

4. <u>Work it out</u> – Exercise as much as you are able. This releases endorphins, which are "happy chemicals" our bodies naturally make when we exercise. Walking can be beneficial in giving energy where needed.

These healing options are practical things to try. They are designed to help. You are changed by grief. God has created you to be creative also and that can help heal your broken heart. God brings healing to both physical and emotional pain. Jesus is a Specialist in this!

<u>Pray:</u> Sometimes this grief journey seems impossible, Lord. I don't feel like I will ever come close to healing. I feel so broken inside. I do see that You can heal my body. Lord, help me have that same confidence that You will heal my heart and emotions. I pray this for today. It's too big to think beyond today. I need help for today! Today I hope and trust that You will heal me in this process.

CrossRoads for Thought:

- *Pick a person to discuss the four "outs" with and talk about which ones you might choose to do. If this person is one of your "safe" people, talk about how you might be accountable to that person in some of these four areas.*
- *Experiment with one or more of the three journaling options to see if that helps. If journaling to God, try beginning with Psalm 1 and using the Psalms daily to journal and meditate. Keep journaling if it helps you process your pain.*
- *Where has God been faithful to heal you in the past? Reflect on both physical and emotional healing that God has provided for you. Spend time in praise to Him as you recall His faithfulness. Pray about the areas that still need His healing touch. Ask another Christian to join you in prayer.*

More Scriptures: Ps 34:18; Ps 147:3; Is 57:18; Jam 5:16; 1 Pet 2:24

25. HEAVEN
– the eternal dwelling place of God

<u>Revelation 21:2</u> *"I saw the Holy City, the new Jerusalem, coming down out of heaven from God, prepared as a bride beautifully dressed for her husband" (NIV).*

*I*t's a day of expectation and great excitement. Much planning, spending, and anticipation occurs before the day. I've experienced this as a bride, as a mother of the bride, and as a mother of the bridegroom. I cannot explain the look on my son's face as he anxiously awaited the appearance of his bride. As she turned the corner, he couldn't hold it in. Although many guests were present, there was now an audience of only one. The groom's eyes were fixed on his bride. They teared with emotion as he saw her – beautifully adorned for their special day. There was pride, joy, excitement, anticipation and love. The appointed time they both longed for had arrived. My world stopped as I witnessed his look. What love!

There is another wedding day coming that we'll witness together. John writes in Revelation 19: 6-9, "'Hallelujah! For our Lord God Almighty reigns. Let us rejoice and be glad and give him glory! For the wedding of the Lamb has come, and his bride has made herself ready. Fine linen, bright and clean, was given her to wear.' (Fine linen stands for the righteous acts of the saints.) Then the angel said to me, 'Write this: Blessed are those who are invited to the wedding supper of the Lamb!' And he added, 'These are the true words of God.'"

For those who have been justified (made right with God through Jesus the Savior), eternal life begins at the moment of spiritual birth. When we pass from this life to the next the Scriptures teach that our souls live eternally. The justified in Christ have eternal life in heaven. Those without Christ are eternally separated from God.

Throughout the Scriptures, both Old and New Testaments, there is the imagery of the wedding. Weddings and marriage are earthly examples that illustrate the intimate relationship between God and His people. In this Scripture John refers to Jesus as the Lamb of God (John 1:29) who gave His life for His Bride, the Church. Death and sin are defeated. It will be a time of great celebration. Believers from all nations will be joined corporately together as the bride of Christ. We will stand with Jesus having exchanged our filthy rags of unrighteousness for the fine linen, bright and clean, given to us to wear. That's how you get invited to the wedding supper. Nothing you do will earn it. It's freely given by the Bridegroom – His righteousness in exchange for your unrighteousness, His clean linen for your filthy rags.

The Greek for "wedding supper" is *"gamos"* - *"a wedding or marriage festival, a wedding banquet, a wedding feast"* (Blue Letter Bible, *"gamos"*). It will be a glorious wedding feast in celebration of that long awaited day.

Eternal life in heaven has been won. That's what heaven is – living eternally with God who created us to have a love relationship forever. John says more about this eternal life in heaven in Revelation 21. There will be a new heaven and a new earth. He says, "I saw the Holy City, the new Jerusalem, coming down out of heaven from God, prepared as a bride beautifully dressed for her husband. And I heard a loud voice from the throne saying, 'Now the dwelling of God is with men, and he will live with them. They will be his people, and God himself will be with them and be their God. He will wipe every tear from their eyes. There will be no more death or mourning or crying or pain, for the old order of things has passed away'" (Revelation 21:2-4). *"Heaven"* is the Greek *"ouranos"* - *"the seat of order of things eternal and consummately perfect where God dwells and other heavenly beings"* (Blue Letter Bible, *"ouranos"*).

What great comfort these words bring to those who grieve. No more death, mourning, crying, or pain. What great relief to be free from this world of sin and hurt. What great relief to know that a loved one has passed into eternal life with God. Death has been defeated for all who are believers. Death has no hold on believers. We need not fear it (1 Corinthians 15:54-57). What comfort this brings as we think about our future with God. You can have this confidence.

ATTENTION! All about heaven and passing through physical death are not fully revealed in Scripture. We know only in part, then we shall know fully (1 Corinthians

13:12). A challenge, with something not fully revealed in the Word, is that sometimes a grieving person can fall prey to what others say about death and heaven. It may be just an opinion. Satan is the great deceiver who twists the truth of God's Word, even with false signs and wonders (2 Thessalonians 2:9). His ways haven't changed since Adam and Eve. He waits to steal, kill, and destroy (John 10:10). If something doesn't sound biblical, even if it sounds good and comforting, turn from it. God's Word doesn't change and it alone is truth.

Some strange books are written about heaven and are not helpful to read. Does it align with God's truth? If not, throw it out. Read God's Word and go to Him with your pain. Avoid mediums and those who claim to connect with the spirits of deceased loved ones. While some of them are simply phonies, others can tap into supernatural powers that are not from God. They are dangerous and must be avoided (Isaiah 8:19-20; Leviticus 19:31; Deuteronomy 18:10-14). Test the spirits to see if they are from God (1 John 4:1-6). Consult a trusted biblical friend or a reputable Bible teacher, especially if you are unfamiliar with God's truth in these areas.

Only the truth of Scripture will carry on into heaven. We know God is revealed through Jesus His Son. We know Jesus through the Word, which God gave us to reveal Himself. Jesus said, "Anyone who has seen me has seen the Father" (John 14:9). He also said, "I am the way and the truth and the life. No one comes to the Father except through me" (John 14:6).

We Christians spend so much time focused on earth, but heaven is our home. We are just aliens and strangers passing through (1 Peter 2:11). While we have genuine pain and grief in this life, the hurt will end. Praise God! But don't miss this point: An end to hurt is coming to the ones invited to the wedding supper. Have you received God's gift in Jesus as your Savior? If you have, praise God. Your time on earth is short in comparison to the glory yet to come. God's love is His gift to others also. It's never too late for you or anyone to trust in Jesus as Lord and Savior. There is a place for you at the wedding feast to come through Jesus.

At that moment when I saw my son at his wedding, I couldn't help but think about the reality of that day that lies ahead for all believers. As I watched my son's eyes, God gave me a picture of His heart for me...and you. I couldn't help but picture the eyes of my Savior at that day yet to come. I know it will be that same look, magnified times a million. As Jesus the Bridegroom awaits His bride (the Church), I can only imagine the look that will be in His eyes. I imagine it so full of love and expectation.

That day of rejoicing is coming. You can only imagine the loving Father watching His Son waiting for His bride. When times are hard and the grief is severe, picture that wedding feast.

Pray: Thank You, Lord! Thank You for heaven. While earthly life is full of both joy and sorrow, I want to focus on the eternal. I want to focus on heaven where there is an end to the grief, hurt, and pain. I want to remember that You have rescued me from sin. I have life eternal with You. A heavenly home awaits me, fashioned for me by You. I am waiting to see You, Jesus, in joyful and eternal celebration. I can't imagine how You can love me so much but I look forward to all eternity for some degree of understanding.

CrossRoads for Thought:

- *Contemplate Jesus as the Bridegroom awaiting His Bride, the Church. Imagine the celebration that will come. What thoughts do you have that you can apply to your grief?*
- *All of earthly life is pointing to this future day of salvation in heaven. When viewed from a heavenly perspective, earthly life has such a temporal focus. Who do you know that needs to be reminded of this? How can you witness about your future home of heaven even though you presently grieve?*
- *Have you lost your focus of heaven by not taking your grief to God? Spend some time in confession to God. List any ways that you have avoided Him by going to other sources that are contrary to Scripture. Pray and ask for God's forgiveness. Then ask for His protection of your spirit and cling only to His truth.*

More Scriptures: Is 65:17-19; 2 Cor 5:1; Phil 2:10-11; Phil 3:20-21; 2 Tim 1:9-10; 2 Pet 3:8-13

26. HURT
–to make sorrowful, to affect with sadness, cause grief, to throw into sorrow (Also HURTING)

John 21:17 *The third time he said to him, "Simon son of John, do you love me?" Peter was hurt because Jesus asked him the third time, "Do you love me?" He said, "Lord, you know all things; you know that I love you." Jesus said, "Feed my sheep" (NIV).*

Sticks and stones may break my bones, but words will never hurt me! Surely you've heard that old saying. You may have said it back in response to someone. If you did say it, perhaps it was during your growing up years when kids said downright mean things. It's a tough comeback when someone is making fun of you. But is it true? Do words never hurt us?

Well, you know the answer to that question is, "Of course words can be wounding. They can hurt!" The Bible says in Proverbs 18:21, "The tongue has the power of life and death." How true! Once words are said, they can't be taken back and they often stick in our memory. Can they be forgiven? Of course, but they do make their impression once spoken aloud. Certain wounding words can take years to be freed from their ill effects.

Good communication can be tricky. When you add in grief it just escalates the challenge of communicating in a clear, healthy way. Often the bereaved person is hurt by a comment or question of someone who did not intend to cause hurt. It may be a caring remark intended to lessen the pain such as "John is in a much better place now." Or it could be words telling a person how to feel such as "She wouldn't want you to wallow in your pain. Just don't think about it." Or they care and want to take your pain away and fix it. They assume and make a declaration such as "I know it will be best for you to get out every day so I'm going to pick you up for lunch." I'm sure you could write some of your own. These words, rather than helping, often hurt.

Why do statements that are meant to help do just the opposite? It isn't about what <u>others</u> think is right for you; it is about what <u>you</u> feel. You may want just their presence and safety of "being with" and accompanying you while you grieve. On some days lack of words or even silence can be the most helpful. It's hard enough to just function on some days, let alone the pressure of expectations of how others think you should be grieving. It is better to have honest statements such as "I have no idea what you are feeling, but does it help to just have me be with you today?" "Is it OK to ask if you have some supportive help?" "How can I best help you?" "Do you want to talk?" "Do you want me to just listen?" "Can I do something for you?" "Is there anything that needs to be done?" The idea is that it is about your needs, not others' ideas or perceived expectations of what they think you should be doing. You need to express what you think. You need listeners. That is what you need.

In John 21:15-19 Peter is talking with the resurrected Christ. Three times Jesus asked Peter if he truly loved Him. After he answered two times, "Yes, Lord, you know that I love you," Peter was hurt that Jesus asked him the third time. The KJV uses the words, "Peter was grieved." The Greek *"lypeō"* means *"to make sorrowful; to affect with sadness, cause grief, to throw into sorrow"* (Blue Letter Bible, *"lypeō"*). The three times no doubt reminded Peter of the three times he had denied Christ before He was crucified. Jesus had warned Peter this would happen. I can only imagine how this third question suddenly "lypeo" – "threw Peter into sorrow" about his failure. Yet with the third one Jesus affirmed Peter's confession of love for Him and the future apostolic work of his ministry. Peter was forgiven and restored. Although Jesus' words to Peter hurt initially, He was doing a deeper work of healing in Peter that prepared him for his mission.

What causes those most hurtful times for you? It can be those statements that mean well but fall short. For the people who repeatedly err in this way you may have to put up boundaries for contact to be limited. Stick to your "safe people" who understand you, care, and aren't trying to "fix" you. This applies to family contacts as well as friends.

Have you experienced the hurt of silence? People don't know what to do or say so they choose to do nothing. They avoid you. You have heard nothing from them since the funeral. This can be the most wounding. Most people can identify family or friends who fall into this category. You may be so hurt by them that now you are not wanting any contact with them. Go to the Lord and process this hurt.

Another hurtful thing is that friendships and relationships can shift after death. This can be unsettling, but it is the reality of how things can change. Some friendships can become more precious, while others dissolve because they are just too awkward.

Do you also have certain "triggers" that bring the torrent of hurt? Often they are connected to the five senses. You can be having an OK grief day and then suddenly it can be what you see, hear, touch, smell, or taste that throws you into sorrow. It brings back a memory of your loved one in a particular way. Some examples: it may be you smell her favorite cologne on someone else; you touch the favorite chair he sat in; you hear your favorite song on the radio; you sing the song at church that you both loved; you taste the pumpkin pie your neighbor brought over that tastes just like the one your wife baked at Thanksgiving; you see the mushrooms in the store that your husband loved. You weren't planning on having such memories but they are "triggered" and the missing of him or her intensifies with the sensual interaction.

You may see that you have hurt someone else by what you have said or done. If so, go and ask forgiveness. That will bring healing. Both parties will be helped.

Words can hurt you, but they also can bless you. You have the power to bless or curse with your words. You can give life to another by blessing or you can drain life from another by your negative or hurtful words. Be mindful of what you choose.

Pray: *Lord, this is so hard. I've been hurt by others. I know it. They've let me down and haven't been there. Some just say stupid things. I know I've also said some things I shouldn't have in my pain. I felt alone. I'm sorry. I've sinned. As You forgive me, help me to forgive others. I can't do it without Your help. To want to forgive them requires help. I'm asking You for that help.*

CrossRoads for Thought:

- *What "triggers" have you experienced so far? What senses were involved? Write them down so you can begin to understand the connection.*
- *Who has spoken blessing into your life? Who has spoken words that were not healing? Can you foster the healthy relationships and put up healthy boundaries for the negative relationships?*
- *How has God forgiven you? Is there someone you need to ask forgiveness? Is there someone you need to offer forgiveness? Pray and let God search your heart. Meet, call, or write anyone He shows you. This is a BIG step for healing along your grief journey.*

More Scriptures: Prov 10:19; Mt 6:12; Jn 16:20; Col 3:13; 1 Pet 1:3-7; 1 Jn 1:9

27. JOY
–gladness

<u>Hebrews 12:2</u> *Fixing our eyes on Jesus, the author and perfecter of faith, who for the joy set before Him endured the cross, despising the shame, and has sat down at the right hand of the throne of God (NASB).*

Ready, set, go! The gun goes off. The race has started. I've had the joy of watching my children run track. They were all fast runners. One of them, a sprinter/jumper, set records during her track and field years in college. What joy seeing her cross over that finish line in first place. She was the winner! What focus, determination, and training it took for the brief 60 or the 100 meter race. But what satisfaction and joy are derived by crossing that finish line and knowing all the hard work, training, determination and focus paid off by winning first prize.

Every two years our world comes together at the Olympics to watch the best athletes compete. Nation against nation, participants compete in races and contests to see which country can win the most medals, especially the gold. Who will finish as the best in the competition?

Does your grief journey ever feel like you are running a race? It is not a competition to see who will be first or get the gold. Instead it is a twisting, turning road you are running. You didn't want to get into this race, but here you are. You just want to get out and quit, but you can't. You are tired, worn out – physically and emotionally. Where is the finish line? Will this grief journey ever be done?

Paul was familiar with the Greek athletic assemblies and their national games in the great amphitheaters. Several times he uses athletic imagery, applying it to living the Christian faith. While you run the race marked out for you, you know it is not a short sprint like my daughter ran. This is a long-distance race. The Greek language uses the word for "race" (*"agōn"*) - *"the assembly of the Greeks at their national games; generally, any struggle or contest; a battle"* (Blue Letter Bible, *"agōn"*). Here you see the root word from which we get our English word "agony." At times living the Christian walk of faith is a journey full of both joy and agony. Your life has spiritual battles. As a Christian you know that your life will not be exempt from trials and hurts. How true, especially in times of deep grief when you feel the agony or experience the hardest times in this Christian journey.

Yet Paul gives you truths that you can apply to the Christian life, especially during times of endurance and struggle. First, he reminds you why there is a need for a race. It is all about love, lived out for you by Jesus. Jesus is not only the perfect example, but He is also the author and perfecter of your faith. Hebrews 12:2 says of Jesus, "Who for the joy set before Him endured the cross" (NASB). There are three words for joy in the New Testament. Here the Greek word for "joy" is *"chara,"* meaning *"joy, glad-ness; the cause or occasion of joy - of persons who are one's joy"* (Blue Letter Bible, *"chara"*). How could Jesus say that there was "joy" before Him as He was getting ready to endure the cross and its shame?

Jesus was well aware of the horror of the cross but the great joy beyond that horror was the reason He came – to rescue sinners. Ahead of Him lay the victory over death and sin for us by His endurance. Satan would be defeated. Jesus would reign with God at His right hand. He had an eternal heavenly focus, motivated by His love for us. Eternal redemption for mankind and His glorification were the objects of "joy" set before Him. Christ's death was for you, and you are His "joy." I am His "joy." When Jesus was on His way to the cross, He knew what was ahead. But He went with joy because of His great love for His Father and His redeemed.

Second, Paul tells you how to run this race. Surrounded by the great cloud of witnesses who have gone before us, you are to throw off everything that hinders and the sin that so easily entangles, and run with perseverance the race marked out for you. Running this Christian race of life requires awareness of sin that can entangle you. Other things may need to be thrown off that aren't sin but yet they can hinder you. You must "fix your eyes on Jesus" as you run this race. The Greek for "fixing our eyes" is *"aph-oraō" - "to turn the eyes away from other things and fix them on something"* (Blue Letter Bible, "aphoraō"). You can understand this to be the single focus, as the runner concentrates only on the finish line to win the prize. Your single-minded focus involves a "turning away from" and a "turning to." Learn what you need to turn away from. What is now hindering you? How can you turn to Jesus?

It's all about Jesus. He is the author of your faith and He is what your life and faith are about. You are part of the corporate "joy" He envisioned before He endured the cross. He is the "joy" you see at the completion of the race. He helps you with strength to endure to the end.

Third, the word for "joy" *("chara")* is very close in etymology to the Greek word for "grace" *("charis")* (Blue Letter Bible, *"charis"*). It is interesting to note that both joy and grace are gifts from God. They are not gifts that you produce, but can only come from outside yourself. They are the work of the Spirit. Only the Christian faith has the paradox of being able to endure pain, grief, and sadness, while knowing joy in the midst of it. It is a deep abiding place of peace and love rooted in God alone.

There are five ways that can help you find joy.

1. Recognize you join a throng of believers who have gone before us from whom you can learn by their examples. If your loved one died as a believer in Christ, he or she is part of that great cloud of witnesses. What comfort and joy that gives. One day you will experience eternal life with them in the presence of God.
2. Remember that while your suffering can feel like forever, it will not be. That is such good news – hopeful news. Yes, it hurts now. But hope comes

as you work through the hurts. You will live through this. Take it one step at a time. Life and its pain will one day end. You are not trapped with sin and hurt. Hallelujah!

3. You must make a conscious decision to take your eyes off of the present circumstances. Remember it is a "turning away" – a looking away from something, recognizing that your pain of grief is a reality – yet, choosing not to dwell there. Express it, but then choose to "turn to" the eternal. Dwell on the future reality yet to come and how you can make a difference today with joy.

4. God is working a maturity in your life as you persevere on this race. As your faith is tested and grows, there is a joy for what God is bringing forth in your life as an example to others, as well as a completion of your faith (James 1:2-4). Joy is for now and the future.

5. As you take your eyes off of your present hurts, you look beyond the hurts to the future prize. What joy and celebration awaits at the finish line. You win because Christ has won for you (James 1:12).

God has given the means to running this Christian race; He is the Giver of grace and joy. Since Jesus is the Trainer, you are the recipient of grace and joy. He develops them in you as you humbly submit to His training. What joy Jesus must have as your joy in Him finds its expression during your hardest times of endurance. The race is worth the future joy. Your eyes must be fixed on the prize. You are getting closer.

Pray: I seem as far from joy as I can be right now, Lord. While I look forward to that future joy where there will be no more pain or sorrow, today that is not my reality. I want Your joy. I can't do this alone. Train me gently, Lord, but work through my pain and grief to change my character. Bring me a peace that passes understanding and a joy to know I'm in Your care. You are the trainer who is preparing me for Your glory. It just hurts. I'm so thankful that You are my strength and joy. Help me focus on You alone, Lord.

CrossRoads for Thought:

- *Is sin entangling your grief journey and robbing you of joy? What do you need to throw off that is hindering you to draw near to Jesus, your source of joy? He sits at the right hand of God, interceding for you. Turn to Jesus. Will you pray to Him?*

- *Make note of family members who live/lived their lives for Jesus. How do/did you see them finding "joy" in the Christian race? What did they endure? What do/did they do that makes them different? Read Hebrews 11. Make note of the great throng of believers who have gone before you. If you have more time, read each story (in the Old Testament) found in Hebrews 11 and meditate on all of them, asking God where these heroes of the faith found "joy."*

- *Just as you can turn to Jesus, He may have you turn to help others. When you help others, it minimizes your own pain and maximizes your joy. Pray and ask God who might need your help. Decide what you can do. Will you do it anonymously or will they know? Picture how your help will bless them and give you joy. Then do it.*

<u>More Scriptures:</u> Ps 126:5; Jn 16:20-22; Rom 5:2b-5; Rom 15:13; Gal 5:22; James 1:2-4, 12

28. LOSS
–damage

Philippians 3:7-11 *But whatever was to my profit I now consider loss for the sake of Christ. What is more, I consider everything a loss compared to the surpassing greatness of knowing Christ Jesus my Lord, for whose sake I have lost all things. I consider them rubbish, that I may gain Christ and be found in him, not having a righteousness of my own that comes from the law, but that which is through faith in Christ – the righteousness that comes from God and is by faith. I want to know Christ and the power of his resurrection and the fellowship of sharing in his sufferings, becoming like him in his death, and so, somehow, to attain to the resurrection of the dead (NIV).*

I've played many games, and most people who know me know I am very competitive. I don't like to lose. Most people don't. Some have a fit and get ugly if they lose. But some are better losers than others. They lose graciously and congratulate the winner. Sometimes winning has more to do with the simple satisfaction of being declared "the winner." At other times winning has to do with the attainment of something valuable, such as money, a title, or a position.

Talking about losing a game or contest doesn't compare to the loss of a loved one. I've noticed some people don't like the usage of the word "loss." They might say, "I didn't *lose* my loved one. It was death." How true, but with the death there is an incredible loss of a lot of things.

Depending on the type of relationship lost (parent, spouse, sibling, child, or friend), there will be other losses that the bereaved experiences. If a child loses a parent, the child might feel the loss of having someone older and wiser or that there are no grandparents for his or her children. If a person loses a spouse, he or she feels the loss of companionship, sexual intimacy, the cook, the financial person, the caring parent, or the fix-it person. If a parent loses a child, there is the loss of seeing the child grow up, going to school, and having an adult life. For each type of relationship, every one of these roles and others like them can be felt as a loss.

The death of a loved one is challenging. It is continually walking through the loss of what was reality and the anticipated future. That is what death is. When each individual loss is felt it magnifies the intensity of the feelings.

I love where Paul takes us in his comparative analysis. EVERYTHING is a "loss" (Greek *"zēmia"* - *"damage, loss"*) (Strong 659, "loss") compared to the greatness of knowing Jesus as his Savior. All else in life is rubbish in order to gain Christ and be found in Him.

These are strong words when we are hurting and grieving. We have real feelings that matter to God. They aren't rubbish. What Paul meant is that life on earth is about gaining Christ and knowing Him. The Greek word *"ginōskō"* that Paul uses for "know" (Blue Letter Bible, *"ginisko"*) correlates with the same word in Hebrew that was used in Genesis when Adam "knew" (*"yada"* KJV) (Blue Letter Bible, *"yada"*) Eve. It designates a deep intimacy. What Paul had in mind is this: When we see life on earth as primarily about our relationship with Christ and growth in intimacy with Him, then all other experiences don't compare to the greatness of being found in Him. It's that simple and that hard – all at the same time.

Being in Christ is a gift of God. It is not something you have to work hard to earn. Jesus paid the price for sins on the cross. It is a gift that you can receive. It is received by faith. Thanks be to God.

Did Paul have no empathy for the bereaved? Quite the contrary, he did. Few, if any, have resumes of suffering like his (2 Corinthians 11:23-29). He had been in prison, flogged, beaten, stoned, shipwrecked, hungry, thirsty, cold, naked, and tired with other life challenges. He had solid ground to talk about grief. When you think about the loss through the lens of Scripture, remember Paul. Even though the deep loss of one you love is great, it does not compare to the greatness of knowing Christ and growing in Him. The greatness of knowing Christ Jesus as Lord is to "gain Christ and be found in him" (see Philippians 3:8-9).

Paul said he wanted to know Christ, the power of His resurrection, and the fellowship of sharing in His sufferings, becoming like Him in his death. Christ exhibited the ultimate servant heart in doing all that the Father asked Him to do. He was obedient unto death. That is the goal.

So what does being found in Christ look like for the bereaved? It involves having this same obedient heart toward the Father and trusting His ways. No one who loves wants to experience the loss of a loved one. But we can see that this death experience is a way to grow in our gaining of Christ and being found in Him. It is a way to know Him more intimately and share in the fellowship of His sufferings. By that we learn the greatness of knowing Christ in new ways. Are they ways we would have chosen? No! But are they ways the Lord can use to grow us in Him? Yes!

I like to win, but I desire to lose all things to gain Christ. This is my heart's desire. This means putting any relationship I have in His loving hands and trusting His ways for me. May He be glorified in your life as you suffer this loss to gain Christ and be found in Him.

Pray: Lord, this loss is severe. I would never have chosen it. Now I choose to trust Your ways for me in the midst of the pain. I want to know You more, Lord. Help me and change me to be more like You, Lord. I want to gain You alone. May others see You in me.

CrossRoads for Thought:

- *Can you identify many of the individual losses that have come with the death of your loved one? Reflect and write them out so that you can begin to recognize where feelings of loss can surface unexpectedly.*
- *How does comparing your sufferings to that of Christ's sufferings encourage you on your grief journey?*
- *How does an eternal perspective of being found in Christ help you deal with the loss?*

More Scriptures: Ps 73:25; Jn 17:3; 1 Cor 3:10-15; Eph 4:13; Phil 3:13-14; 1 Pet 4:12-13

29. OVERWHELMED
–to languish, to faint, used of the soul, or spirit

<u>Psalm 142:1-3</u> *I cry out to the Lord with my voice; With my voice to the Lord I make my supplication. I pour out my complaint before Him; I declare before Him my trouble. When my spirit was overwhelmed within me, Then You knew my path. In the way in which I walk They have secretly set a snare for me (New King James Version).*

*H*ave you ever been in a situation where you were overcome and fainted? What a helpless feeling. Fainting is actually something our bodies do to help us survive. "If blood and oxygen levels in the brain drop too low, the body immediately starts shutting down nonvital parts to direct resources to vital organs. When the brain detects lower levels of oxygen, breathing will speed up to increase the levels. The heart rate will also increase, so that more oxygen reaches the brain. This reduces blood pressure in other parts of the body. The brain then receives extra blood at the expense of other body areas" (Felman n.pag). It is scary. How good of God to make our bodies in such a way that during an overwhelming crisis, the body responds to a higher order for functioning.

You have probably noticed with the crisis of death and grief, that your body is greatly affected. Grief is so overwhelming. There are many common symptoms that are typical of those in beginning grief. Perhaps you have the "foggy thinking." This is when concentration is greatly affected and you can't remember where you put things, who you talked to, and what was said. Some people are so overwhelmed that they actually begin to believe they are losing their minds. Don't worry – odds are you aren't. This is how grief can exhibit itself.

Overwhelmed may not be a strong enough word to describe the actual feelings accompanying grief. Experiencing this grief journey may be the hardest thing you will ever do. That's why you find so much comfort in God's Word in many of the Psalms. I encourage you to read the Psalms while you are in grief. They are loaded with feelings from real people like you and me. And the real people went to the real God who is able to listen and act. Many of the Psalms were written by King David, others by several singers or musicians. Some are songs composed primarily for a book of prayer and praise. Many are poetical in style. The author, whether David or another, collectively referred to as "the Psalmist," prayed to God about real life situations. They are loaded with emotions that are related to yours.

Many of the Psalms are Psalms of Lament. Roughly 65 - 67 of the 150 Psalms fit into this category. Psalms of lament deal in portion or entirety with calling out to God in the midst of extreme situations. God in His wisdom let these laments be a part of His Word. Other portions of God's

Word include lamenting sections, most notably the books of Job and Lamentations.

Psalm 142 is ascribed to David and is a deliverance prayer written when he was in a cave being pursued by his enemy. He was alone and felt forsaken by all. He cried out to the Lord and poured out his "complaint" (*"siyach"*) to Him. The Hebrew word here points to his pouring out his *"quarrel"* to God (Blue Letter Bible, *"siyach"*). David declared before God his struggle and his trouble.

What the lamenting Psalms show is that you can go to God, recognizing that He is your only help. He is your refuge and your safe place when you are in desperate need. He can handle your struggles and honest feelings. It is a gift to go to Him when you hurt or are troubled.

David declared, "When my spirit was overwhelmed within me, Then You knew my path" (Psalm 142:3 NKJV). The Hebrew for "overwhelmed" (*"`ataph"*) - *"to languish, to faint, used of the soul, or spirit"* (Blue Letter Bible, *"ataph"*) reminds me of the extreme conditions just before fainting. There is a darkness of emotions associated with this that can cause fainting. David recognized that his spirit was growing faint and was about to be overwhelmed. He calls out to God to voice his complaint before he is totally overwhelmed. He in essence "faints into the arms of God."

God knows how overwhelmed and desperate we are when we are hurting, confused, or in trouble. He knows how complex the feelings with grief can be. He knows that sometimes we are even angry and upset with Him. Even when we think He is the source of our trouble or that He isn't listening to us or that He even cares, we can go to Him and acknowledge these real feelings. We aren't missing God when we do this. We are "fainting into his loving arms" for Him to give us exactly what we need. We are acknowledging that He is the only source of strength when we are weak and about to give up. When we are weak, He is strong.

What is the opposite of going to God with your laments and feelings of being overwhelmed? It is listening to lies. You can substitute any enemy of the Psalmist with the real enemy of your soul, Satan. The believer in Christ is in a constant spiritual battle with the forces of darkness. "Your enemy the devil prowls around like a roaring lion looking for someone to devour. Resist him, standing firm in the faith" (1 Peter 5:8-9a). As the enemy set a snare for David, Satan wants to snare you. He speaks his lies to you to convince you that God took your loved one because He doesn't care about you. He wants you to give up. He wants to take you out. He wants to make you doubt God and be ineffective as a witness of His grace. How good to know that Satan himself has been snared and defeated by Jesus.

Jesus your Savior also experienced overwhelming sorrow. In Matt 26:38 He said, "My soul is overwhelmed with sorrow to the point of death." He died and rose from His grave, conquering sin and overwhelming death. He understands pain and sorrow. Go to Him and pour out your complaint and troubles. He is your Rescuer and Refuge. "Set me free from my prison, that I may praise your name" (Psalm 142:7). Death and sin have been defeated. Praise

His name! Go to Him and faint into His arms when you are overwhelmed.

Pray: *I'm here, Lord, but I'm so overwhelmed I can hardly function. Thank You, Lord, that I can be honest with You. It's hard to know sometimes what I feel. I find great comfort to know that as I come, acknowledging my emptiness, You will receive me. You understand me and know my path. You know where the enemy would place a snare. Help me trust You, Lord, and never doubt. Help me silence the lies of the enemy where he would discourage me. Thank You, Jesus, for understanding sorrow. Your love for me caused You to die for me. Thank You that when I am weak and faint Your arms of love catch me and hold me tight.*

CrossRoads for Thought:

- *Before a person becomes overwhelmed, there are warning signs. Have others expressed some statements of concern for you? Is there truth in their statements? What are some warnings God may be showing you so that you are not overcome?*

- *Be honest with God. Lament when you need to. Journal your real feelings to Him, recognizing He is your safe place. Be open as God may lead you into times of confession or repentance as well as times of worship. As you position yourself before Him to be honest, quiet your spirit to hear from Him.*

- *What would it look like for Jesus to be "overwhelmed with sorrow to the point of death?" How would this sorrow affect His appearance? His Spirit? Picture Jesus loving you so much that He chose this. How will you praise His name today?*

More Scriptures: Ps 77:1-15; Ps 102:1-2; Is 57:15-16

30. REGRET
–to care afterwards (Also REGRETFUL)

<u>2 Corinthians 7:8-9</u> *"Even if I caused you sorrow by my letter, I do not regret it. Though I did regret it – I see that my letter hurt you, but only for a little while – yet now I am happy, not because you were made sorry, but because your sorrow led you to repentance" (NIV).*

It's amazing how technology has changed our lives. I can't imagine what things will be like in 20 years. Take for example the invention of the television. Since its arrival in the mid 1900's, we have continued to see changes. From the days of black and white to the colors that brighten our screens, things have significantly improved. One feature I like is the ability to record what I can't watch. How great it is to watch those shows at later times. And I can fast forward, skip, pause and replay what I want to see more carefully. I can delete anything by the touch of two buttons. Ah, the blessings of technology!

Do you wish a grief journey had a fast forward button or a delete button? "If only…." "What if…?" "I only wish…" These are so normal. Regrets are common with your grief journey. If not dealt with, they can hinder the healing steps in your process. It can feel like you are stuck in that "pause and rewind" mode, caught replaying the same thing over and over.

There is a close relationship between regret and guilt. Let me differentiate for clarity purposes.

- Regrets are the things you wish you had said or done.
- Guilt is what you feel when you believe you have done something wrong (Fitzgerald 92).

Some typical examples after the death of a loved one are:
"I only wish I had told him I loved him more often."
"If only I could have seen her again before she died."
"What if I had gotten him in to see the doctor sooner?"
"If only I had been driving the car that day!"
These types of statements are common, especially in the beginning days of grief. While guilt can be a more intense emotion than regret, they both can cause great distress.

This is the time to be compassionate to yourself. It is normal to review things in your mind. It is easy to forget the extreme emotional stress you may have been under as a caregiver. You may question why you missed something. Hindsight is always easier, but it isn't the same as the reality of the situation at that time. No person or relationship is perfect. There are things you said or did that you wish you could go back and change. But you can't. Trust in the Lord and leave them with Him.

You may choose to express these regrets to friends or family. This can be a good thing; it can also be a risk. Some may respond back to you something like, "Oh! Don't feel that way." While they mean well, that statement doesn't help. You need to express your feelings, but not be given judgment. Sometimes clarity can come by discussing regretful feelings with a compassionate listener. It is one thing to listen with a heart to hear and walk along beside. It is another thing to listen and tell someone what to think, feel, or explain away the feelings. Find the right listener – a "safe" person.

Paul wrote about regret. He had written to the church at Corinth. He had needed to address some things for correction and clarity. While he regretted that he had to write a hard letter, in 2 Corinthians 7:8-9 he wrote that he did not regret that his words brought them to sorrow and repentance. The Greek word for "regret" (*"metamelomai"*) meaning *"to care afterwards"* (Blue Letter Bible, *"metamelomai"*) is close in meaning to "repent" (*"metanoeō"*) meaning *"to change one's mind for better, heartily to amend with abhorrence of one's past sins"* (Blue Letter Bible, *"metanoeō"*). In the Synonym Results in the Blue Letter Bible, the distinction given is regret refers to an emotional change and repentance to a change of choice. Regret has reference to particulars and repentance to the entire life. Regret signifies remorse; repentance is the reversal of moral purpose and is expressive of moral action and issues (Blue Letter Bible, *"metamelomai"*).

The slight difference in meaning of these words can bring some practical application into your grief journey and help you deal with regrets. Regret is an emotional change to a particular situation causing remorse, while to a greater degree repentance is a change of the mind to an opposite direction. A practical example is a child who regrets he did something wrong because he was caught. But he isn't truly repentant or sorry for what he did. He is regretful he was caught and that he has to suffer consequences. But his heart didn't change by being caught.

It isn't wrong to process regrets. It's normal grief for most. But it is unhealthy to get stuck there and continue "rewinding." You'll know if you are stuck as you see where your mind dwells and if you become obsessed with regrets. Whatever you have missed is covered by the cross of Jesus. Don't continue to beat yourself up, trapped in unforgiveness of self or others. The answer to unforgiveness is what? Repentance!

How do you do it? Say, *"I'm wrong to hold onto this regret, Lord. (State what your regret is). It is sin and not trusting You. Thank You that You have forgiven me. I choose to forgive myself and others. Show me what I need to learn."*

Warning! Satan likes to try to bring these things back into your "saved recordings." When you see them pop up, delete them right away. You've already done that "regret recording" and God helped you delete it. You don't need to go back to see it again. You know it has been deleted. Your mind has been changed through repentance and forgiveness. Live in the reality that your thinking on this has been changed by God's big delete button. What a powerful God!

Pray: It's so very hard to control these thoughts. I keep thinking about the past, what I wish I had done. It feels like a stuck tape at times. Help me to process this with You, Lord. If I do it by myself, I feel broken. My thinking isn't clear. I've already forgotten how hard some things were and why I made certain decisions. Help me be compassionate with myself when You show me that. Help me see where my regret is hurting me. Keep me from sin.

CrossRoads for Thought:

- *Make a list of any regrets you feel, especially ones that keep recycling in your mind. Differentiate between regrets and guilts (go to "guilt" page for guilts). Begin to journal about each one: why you feel it, what caused it, what action you can take to get rid of it. Allow time to process.*

- *Set up a visit with a Christian friend, Christian pastor, or Christian counselor. Have regrets written down. Discuss any regrets you are experiencing. Ask to help you pray through any need for repentance and forgiveness. Doing it with another person creates a "delete memory" that you can date and remember when it tries to replay.*

- *Processing regrets can bring about repentance for change. Look for any lessons you learned that can make you a better person or help someone else. For example, if you regret not spending enough time with your loved one, commit to spending more time with others you love. If you regret not saying "I love you" more, commit to saying it often to someone.*

More Scriptures: Ps. 103:12; Mk 1:15; Acts 3:19; Acts 26:18; Eph 1:7; 1 Jn 1:9

CONCLUSION

*W*e know that this life is temporary. After passing through it, we Christians will enter eternity with our Savior. As we live on this side of eternity, our experiences include tremendous joys as well as loss and grief. But God doesn't abandon us at the times of our greatest needs. Instead, He provides help through family, friends, church, community, neighbors, prayer, and support groups; above all other means, He provides help through His Word. Although at times we may feel like we will never navigate through the pain of loss, God reminds us, "Never will I leave you; never will I forsake you" (Hebrews 13:5). He has given us everything we need in life through His promised Holy Spirit and His inspired Word. No one can comfort the way God does.

I hope this book has given you a greater understanding of God's truth applied to grief. You have learned common words based upon their original Hebrew and Greek words – without having to learn the languages. The Holy Spirit, the divine Comforter, can bring understanding, healing, and comfort at times when you are feeling loss, confusion, or desperation due to the pain of grief. He can use the truths from these words at various times during the rest of your life, bringing them back to your remembrance when needed.

As you discover greater depth in the inspired Word of God, this accomplishes two things. First, you are better equipped to deal with your own grief. God comforts you. Second, you are also equipped to help others who grieve. You can comfort others as God has comforted you. He says it best in His Word, "Praise be to the God and Father of our Lord Jesus Christ, the Father of compassion and the God of all comfort, who comforts us in all our troubles, so that we can comfort those in any trouble with the comfort we ourselves receive from God" (2 Corinthians 1:3-4). What a loving, caring, and gracious God we have! To God be the glory.

APPENDIX

TOP 30 SURVEY RESPONSES from GRIEF WORDS REQUEST

(In order of frequency mentioned)

17	Hope/ful/less/ness	5	Prayer
15	Lonely/ness	5	Trust
12	Love/ing/d	4	Acceptance
11	Comfort/ing	4	Grief
11	Empty/ness	4	Guilt/y
9	Strength	4	Heal/ing
8	Fail/fullness	4	Heaven
8	Peace	4	Hurt/ing
8	Sad/ness	4	Joy
6	Alone	4	Loss
6	Anger	4	Overwhelmed
6	Fear	4	Regret/ful
6	Sorrow		
6	Tears		
5	Abandon/ment/ed		
5	Despair		
5	Lost		
5	Pain		

WORKS CITED

"Alone." Def. < http://www.merriam-webster.com/dictionary/alone> 6 Jul 2012.

Blue Letter Bible. 1996-2012. 21 Aug 2012. < http:// www.blueletterbible.org/lang/lexicon/lexicon.cfm?Strongs=KJV>.

Easton, Burton Scott. "Hope", *International Standard Bible Encyclopaedia*. Edited by James Orr. Blue Letter Bible. 1913. 5 May 2003 21 Aug 2012. <http://www.blueletterbible.org/Search/Dictionary/viewTopic.cfm?type=GetTopic&Topic=Hope&DictList=4#ISBE>.

Felman, Adam. "What is Fainting, and What Causes It?" *Medical News Today* (July 2019): n. pag. Medical News Today. Web. 26 Oct. 2019

Fitzgerald, Helen. *The Mourning Handbook*. New York: Fireside-Simon & Schuster, Inc., 1994. Print.

"Guilt." Def. <http://dictionary.reference.com/browse/guilt?s=t> 14 Aug 2012.

Guzik, David. "Study Guide for Ephesians 2." Enduring Word. Blue Letter Bible. 7 Jul 2006. 2012. 17 Aug 2012. <http:// www.blueletterbible.org/commentaries/comm_view.cfm?AuthorID=2&contentID=8034&commInfo=31&topic=Ephesians&ar=Eph_2_10 >.

Guzik, David. "Study Guide for Hebrews 13." Blue Letter Bible. 21 Feb, 2017. Web. 6 Dec, 2019. <https://www.blueletterbible.org/Comm/guzik_david/StudyGuide2017-Hbr/Hbr-13.cfm>.

Henry, Matthew. "Commentary on Psalms 119." Blue Letter Bible. 1 Mar 1996. 2012. 19 Jun 2012. <http:// www.blueletterbible.org/commentaries/ comm_view.cfm? AuthorID=4&contentID=1242&commInfo=5&topic= Psalms&ar=Psa_119_176 >.

Hoerber, Robert G., ed. Concordia Self-Study Bible. St. Louis: Concordia Publishing House, 1986. Print.

Jamieson, Robert; A.R. Fausset; and David Brown. "Commentary on 2 Corinthians 4." Blue Letter Bible. 19 Feb 2000. 2012. 5 Jun 2012. <http:// www.blueletterbible.org/commentaries/ comm_view.cfm? AuthorID=7&contentID=2993&commInfo=6&topic= 2%20Corinthians&ar=2Cr_4_8 >.

Jamieson, Robert; A.R. Fausset; and David Brown. "Commentary on Psalm 56." Blue Letter Bible. 19 Feb 2000. 2012. 28 Aug 2012. <http:// www.blueletterbible.org/commentaries/ comm_view.cfm? AuthorID=7&contentID=2417&commInfo=6&topic= Psalms&ar=Psa_56_8 >.

"Mourning." Def. < http://www.merriam-webster.com/ dictionary/mourning> 3 Aug 2012.

"Sadness." Def. <http://www.merriam-webster.com/dic-tionary/sadness> 31 Jul 2012.

Spurgeon, Charles Haddon. "The Comforter." Blue Letter Bible. 18 Apr 2001. 2012. 26 Jun 2012.<http:// www. blueletterbible.org/commentaries/comm_view.cfm? AuthorID=10&contentID=3186&commInfo=15&topic= Sermons&ar=Jhn_14_26 >.

Strong, James. *The New Strong's Exhaustive Concordance of the Bible*. Nashville: Thomas Nelson Publishers, 1984. Print.

Vine, W. E. *Vine's Expository Dictionary of New Testament Words*. Blue Letter Bible. 1940. 24 June, 1996 31 Aug 2012. <http://www.blueletterbible.org/search/Dictionary/viewTopic.cfm?type=GetTopic&Topic=9#Vine's> .

ABOUT THE AUTHOR

*S*haron Zehnder loves to use her gifts of encouragement and teaching to inspire others to grow in their Christian faith. An excellent student of the Scriptures and a faithful prayer warrior, Sharon is used by the Lord in one-on-one settings as well as a presenter to groups of people.

Sharon has worked for twenty years as the Aftercare Director and family service counselor in grief recovery for a large family-owned funeral home. She oversees their care support and facilitates grief support groups. She served the Pastoral Leadership Institute (PLI) at its inception by coordinating the monthly prayer network until she became the Retreat Leader for the Partner Program. She served with the Partner Leadership Team of PLI for ten years. She has spoken at retreats and led workshops at various churches and conferences. She has also taught leadership principles for kingdom growth internationally to pastors and wives through PLI International.

She received her Master of Arts degree in Liberal Studies from Concordia University (Chicago) with a concentration in church and community. She received her Bachelor of Science degree in Child and Family Services from Bowling Green State University (Ohio).

Sharon is the mother of three children and grandmother of five. She is married to Mark Zehnder who serves as a pastor in Omaha, Nebraska.

CPSIA information can be obtained
at www.ICGtesting.com
Printed in the USA
LVHW092223240322
714364LV00012B/84